Story, Song and Spirit

Fun and Creative Worship Services for All Ages

Erika Hewitt

Skinner House Books
Boston

Copyright © 2010 by Erika Hewitt. All rights reserved. Published by Skinner House Books, an imprint of the Unitarian Universalist Association of Congregations, a liberal religious organization with more than 1,000 congregations in the U.S. and Canada, 25 Beacon St., Boston, MA 02108-2800.

Printed in the United States

Cover design by Kathryn Sky-Peck
Cover art Window IV, © Danette English
Text design by Suzanne Morgan

ISBN 1-55896-546-7
978-1-55896-546-1

13 12 11 10
6 5 4 3 2 1

Library of Congress Cataloging-in-Publication Data

Hewitt, Erika A.
 Story, song, and spirit : fun and creative worship services for all ages / Erika A. Hewitt.
   p. cm.
 ISBN-13: 978-1-55896-546-1 (pbk. : alk. paper)
 ISBN-10: 1-55896-546-7 (pbk. : alk. paper) 1. Unitarian Universalist Association—Liturgy—Texts. 2. Public worship. 3. Worship programs. I. Title.
 BX9853.H49 2010
 264'.091—dc22
                    2008040673

Permission is granted to photocopy the scripts of the worship services for use in congregational contexts.

We gratefully acknowledge permission to reprint the following material: "The Camels Speak" by Lynn Ungar, from the December 2003 issue of *Quest* (Church of the Larger Fellowship); "Bridging Prayer," adapted from Donna DiSciullo; "The Creator's Workshop," adapted from "A Little Jar Labeled 'Freedom,'" from *What If Nobody Forgave? And Other Stories*, edited by Colleen M. McDonald (Skinner House Books); "The Right Way to Right Speech," adapted from "The Sign," from *Kibitzers and Fools: Tales My Zayda Told Me*, © 2005 by Simms Taback, used by permission of Viking Children's Books, a Division of Penguin Young Readers Group, a member of Penguin Group (USA) Inc., 345 Hudson St., New York, NY 10014, all rights reserved; "Strong Is What We Make Each Other," adapted from "Hare's Gifts" by Ken Collier, from *Our Seven Principles in Story and Verse: A Collection for Children and Adults* (Skinner House Books); "Take My Hand" by Jen Hazel; "Outlawing Jelly Beans, and Other Injustices," adapted from *The Duke Who Outlawed Jelly Beans and Other Stories* by Johnny Valentine, illustrations by Lynette Schmidt, copyright © 1991, permission to reprint and adapt courtesy of Alyson Books.

Contents

Introduction v

Setting Yourself Up for Success viii

SERVICES FOR THE LITURGICAL YEAR

What Will You Bring to the Feast? (Start of the Church Year)   1

Following Yonder Star (Christmas)   11

The Blue-Green Hills of Earth (Earth Day)   24

Good News, Bad News (Bridging Ceremony)   35

SERVICES FOR ANY TIME

The Creator's Workshop   48

The Right Way to Right Speech   58

Strong Is What We Make Each Other   71

Outlawing Jelly Beans, and Other Injustices   83

Babble   96

Benediction   108

Acknowledgments

This book was written by glorious, mysterious accident. I intended to write *one* worship service for all ages, then I decided to try another… then another… until, eventually, it became a joy, not a chore, to craft worship for all ages. Throughout my early, sloppy efforts, my creative process was fed by Rev. Greg Ward, a true intergenerational pioneer, and by the superlatively graceful and wise Rev. Beth Banks. I'm also grateful to the families of the Unitarian Universalist Church of Davis, California, who unwittingly served as an enthusiastic laboratory for my worship experiments.

When I realized that my surplus of scripts might be useful in book form, I started down the Long Road of Publication, from which some never return. I'm grateful to Mary Benard of Skinner House Books for shepherding this project—and me.

When I asked to adapt their creative works, I gratefully received a YES from Jen Hazel, Simms Taback, and Revs. Ken Collier, Cynthia Johnson, Donna DiSciullo, and Lynn Ungar. I appreciate the generosity of spirit they've extended to me. John Douglas also merits special thanks for being generous with his musical skills.

The solitary practice of writing is often sustained by those dearest to the author. I hereby express my deep love and affection for Gordon Huestis and Rev. Dr. Beth Johnson, who have steadfastly provided me with spiritual fuel, humor, and the loving understanding that exists only between Soul Friends.

Finally, my appreciation goes to the indescribably good people of Live Oak Unitarian Universalist Congregation in Goleta, California. This book exists because of you, my dear ones. In ways both subtle and significant, you shape my creativity and my ministry. Thank you.

Introduction

A few years into my ministry, as I gained confidence in creating and leading worship services for all ages, a funny thing started to happen. Each time I was with a colleague and mentioned a service I'd led, my listener would clutch my arm, and plead, "Can you please give me your service? I want to do multigenerational worship, but I don't know how!" More Unitarian Universalist clergy, religious educators, and congregations are eager for worship services that engage people of all ages, and many are afraid to experiment with this new shape of worship.

Much of our collective anxiety probably arises from the incongruous models we have to work with. Our Protestant tradition is based on a worship model built around "The Word": the heart of the service is often a lengthy sermon that may stir hearts, but is directed at minds. Congregants sing, or read responsively, and perhaps they share joys and sorrows—but, by and large, they sit still and listen. It's not surprising that ministers and religious educators grow nervous when they contemplate adding a dozen or two worshipers with small, wriggling bodies and short attention spans. It's a daunting challenge to craft a message that will speak to congregants at all points along the age spectrum.

My first attempts at multigenerational worship followed a simple formula often found in our congregations: I stretched out the "Story for All Ages," condensed the sermon into a brief homily, and added a fun musical piece to round it all out. None of the elements was qualitatively different from those in the adult service, however, and the results often fell flat. But through a combination of wise mentors, holy boldness, sheer stubbornness, and a long process of trial and error, I stumbled upon a new form of worship that encourages active participation rather than passive listening. Making a juicy story the focal point of the service removed the "veil" separating worship leaders from the congregation, and introduced a thematic arc for every element of the service. The right story can bring Unitarian Universalist theology to life, and creates room for spontaneity, playfulness, and reverence with a touch of irreverence.

Here's why this discovery seems so compelling: Across the country, our congregations are filling up with a new generation of Unitarian Universalists—families with young children. It's not enough, in these times, to provide stimulating sermons for adults and, in some distant wing of the church, solid religious education for their young ones. Rather, families need and deserve shared worship they can experience together, take home, talk about, and learn from.

No matter how fabulous your religious education program, children learn qualitatively different lessons about spirituality when they witness adults feeding their hunger for Spirit. Watching adults moved to tears of sadness or joy—and seeing that these tears are welcome—teaches our little ones the ineffable but essential facts of being in community. There's no moment in which congregations *aren't* embodying values that children readily absorb.

Consider, too, that religious communities are just about the last remaining institutions in our society where children regularly interact with adults who aren't relatives or authority figures. In our fellowship halls, church kitchens, and religious education classrooms, children and youth learn how to be in relationship with people who are one, two, or even eight decades older than they are. Worship is another opportunity to strengthen such relationships.

A carefully created service that engages everyone—kids, young adults, parents, empty-nesters, and elders—enlarges the congregation's sense of itself. It's one thing to church children by inviting them to share in worship for fifteen minutes before they're dismissed to their religious education classes. It's quite another to look around and see a congregation, in its full range of ages, worshiping together for an hour. When a congregation views itself as inviting the full breadth of the human lifespan into its sacred hour, it can also engage in shared ministry outside of worship.

How to Use This Book

Unitarian Universalist congregations differ markedly, in size, liturgical preferences, and culture. Think of each service in this book as a suit that may need to be tailored—tiny darts sewn in here, longer cuffs there—to provide a perfect fit for your community. Every congregation has its own habits, patterns, and traditions. Some of yours will be ripe for experimentation and change. Others provide comfort and stability and should not be tampered with.

Most of each service in this book is scripted, to provide worship leaders and actors with a largely ready-to-use service plan. But there's no rule that you *have* to follow the script. You may decide to ad-lib or inject your own style. Some portions of the service have been left unscripted. These are routine parts of every service—the welcome and the chalice lighting—that are best delivered in the worship leader's own words and in the congregation's preferred way.

Each service begins with an introductory paragraph as well as a quick-glance description of the service and its relative complexity. The description includes roles and preparation.

Some roles require lots of speaking and movement, and therefore preparation, while others can be taken on by volunteers the morning of the service, right from their seats. Those who must attend rehearsal are marked with a star (*) but all the actors should be encouraged to participate. Rehearsals can be fun and build team spirit, even for those who don't need it for their minor roles. In nearly all cases, the gender of the role can be changed—just be sure to change the pronouns accordingly throughout the script.

Each service comes with detailed preparation advice. You'll also find a rating indicating whether the service requires minimal, moderate, or significant preparation. Preparation includes making and obtaining props and costumes, as well as rehearsal.

I hope these services will enliven you and your congregation. I wish you bubbles of laughter, many goosebump moments, and the occasional welling of tears. Most of all, I wish that you and your fellow congregants of all ages leave worship on Sunday morning full of gladness and gratitude, and eager for more.

Setting Yourself Up for Success

If the services in this book were of the "just add water" variety, they wouldn't be worth doing. Think about how much love you put into cooking a meal for good friends. When you go to the trouble of inviting people into your home, chances are you want to offer them something more than a "just add water" meal. Worship becomes vibrant when people are invited to open their hearts and spirits, and an invitation *that* exciting takes some effort, and some intention, to extend. Since these worship services are designed to bring congregations to life in an engaging and reflective way, you'll need to put some time and energy into them. I promise that what you and your worship team put into each service, you'll get back in depth and enthusiasm. Take the time to read the service carefully, either as an individual worship leader or as a team, and consider how to adapt these services to *your* particular congregation.

This chapter offers tips and suggestions to help you with the logistics of planning, address some common challenges and questions, and bring some extra creativity and fun to both the planning and the service itself.

Decide Who's in Charge

There should be a single coordinator for each service, someone to serve as part shepherd and part coach. This person should be identified at least two months before the service. The coordinator can take on a central role in the service, such as the Worship Leader (referred to as simply "Leader" in the services) or the Storyteller, but it's more important that this person oversees communication, fosters a sense of teamwork, and coordinates details.

Schedule Preparation

Once you've chosen a service and a coordinator, you're ready to plan the service's "incubation period" and "birth." Here is a timeline for your work:

- One month in advance: recruit actors; consult with musicians; if a food offering is included, consult with your social justice team.

- Three weeks in advance: meet with the music director to plan the music; schedule the rehearsal and, if applicable, reserve the sanctuary for your rehearsal; begin to brainstorm prop and costume ideas, preferably with other team members.

- Two weeks in advance: gather props and costumes; publicize any necessary information (e.g., "Bring canned goods to our service") in your congregation's bulletin.

- One week in advance: conduct the rehearsal; submit the order of service to the appropriate person (don't forget to include the names of your actors and anyone else whose leadership or teamwork made the service possible!).

- Day of the service: bring an extra copy of the script to the service; make sure that actors arrive early; set up necessary props.

- In the week following the service: Send thank you notes to all who participated in the service; celebrate a job well done! It's also a good idea to take notes about what went well and what may be important to consider the next time.

Recruit Early and with Care

Multigenerational services are a golden opportunity to promote shared ministry, and that begins with the service coordinator. Good shepherds and good coaches know how to exercise their leadership without stepping on too many toes. Begin establishing a spirit of teamwork early by including your music director or accompanist in planning how to weave music into the service.

You might also speak to your congregation's youth group about taking a collective role in the service (see suggestions below about including children and youth in worship). Rev. Elizabeth Banks at the Unitarian Universalist Church of Davis, California, has created a Junior Worship Associates program for their weekly Spirited Worship services. These associates span the grade-school ages, with varied levels of responsibility—from delivering opening words to announcing the offering or introducing joys and sorrows.

Undoubtedly, you'll have ideas about thespians in your congregation who would be perfect, but don't underestimate the power of a generally publicized casting call. There are many gifted people in our congregations. Some of them have yet to reveal their gifts and may need the reassurance of an open invitation to step forward. You may be surprised to discover the hams in your pews.

Consider intentionally extending the invitation to youth and children, or even formalizing a way to involve them. The line between "recruiting" and pressuring children should be walked delicately, however. Many congregations delight in seeing their children and youth during worship; as a result, well-meaning worship planners sometimes ask children to sing or perform without fully explaining what the service will entail, or without allowing the children to voice their discomfort. An anxious child performer can make the rest of the congregation squirm in vicarious discomfort. When you invite children or youth to help lead a worship service, make sure they truly have the desire and the confidence to do so, and bring parents into the loop so that the children will be supported at home.

When it comes to assigning specific roles, you may have to tread an equally delicate line between inclusivity and assembling an effective team. The right person in the right role can lift a service from simple to sublime, so it can be tempting to choose the best speakers and actors. On the other hand, our congregations are active models of acceptance and inclusivity, so you should strive to reflect this in your worship service.

Model transparency with volunteers. For example, you might say, "I was thinking of asking Emma to take the role of Tehmina, but is anyone else drawn to it?" When volunteers request certain roles, be certain they've read the script from beginning to end. If a volunteer isn't suited to the role she wants, call upon the full breadth of your diplomatic skills. Alternatively, try to practice what I affectionately call Radical Trust in the Process. More often than not, when one of my volunteers requests a certain role, it results in a magical fit that's better than anything I could have planned.

Plan the Music

All the services contain suggestions for hymns, most of which are from *Singing the Living Tradition* and *Singing the Journey* (indicated in the services by the acronyms *SLT* and *STJ* respectively). In many cases, the suggested hymns are easily picked up by those too young to read, and those with poor eyesight. Feel free to change the musical selections—but be aware that not all hymns are equally accessible.

As with so many other aspects of worship, your congregation surely has its own practices around music beyond the hymns. Some sing to a piano accompaniment, while others sing to the organ. Your congregation may even enjoy the accompaniment of other instruments and you may want to include them in one of these services. Because the services are meant to set a welcoming, less formal tone, they will likely feel more cohesive if you choose instruments that fit that tone. By their very nature (and with no disrespect intended), instruments such as a piano, guitar, or set of drums sound less formal than an organ, cello, or violin.

In some churches, the hymns are led by the choir director, or even the choir. If your congregation's choir regularly sings during worship, it's even more important to collaborate early with the music or choir director. If the choir plans to sing an anthem on their own, can the anthem fit the service's theme? Can it be interactive? Or, if you know that one of the suggested hymns is unfamiliar, perhaps the choir, music director, or accompanist could teach it to the congregation in the weeks leading up to the big day.

Finally, since the musical cues in these services aren't necessarily obvious, be sure to supply your accompanist and/or music director with a copy of the script so that she or he can follow along.

Use the Space Well

Many churches and fellowships have at least one pulpit and a raised chancel (the area around the pulpit). In general, the stories in these services will be best brought to life if the central characters are in the center of the congregation's view. The Leader and the Storyteller should be off to one side, leaving room for the action to unfold. If the pulpit is moveable, it's easier to create a space in which the service can flow easily. If it's not moveable, consider using a music stand for the Leader and the Storyteller instead. If your sanctuary has moveable chairs, consider holding a short work party to shift them into a configuration that will complement your service—just make sure your rehearsal is held in that configuration as well.

The entrances, actions, and exits of your characters are up to you, the service coordinator. You'll need to put your director hat on top of the shepherd and coach hats you're already wearing. Your stage directions will likely depend on the number and placement of microphones, which are often necessary for dialogue to be heard by all. Actors can share microphones, but the Storyteller and the Leader often need their own, which they can share.

A few services rely on a clearly defined space, which is explained in the "Preparation" section (such as "The Creator's Workshop," which calls for a table and some "shelves"). Most of these services, though, require very little beyond a shared agreement among actors that, for instance, the area next to the piano will be the stable in Bethlehem. There are simple ways to mark locations, or create settings on the spot. For example, the Grand Duke Dwayne's castle "balcony" might be a railing that's carried in front of the actor. Similarly, when characters journey, they might just circle the chancel slowly. No one expects Hollywood sets. People will give their imagination to you with very little prompting.

Collaborate on Props and Costumes

Bringing these services to life is a job for everyone. At the time you line up your actors—about one month before the service—have them read the script and let it tickle their imaginations. Encouraging the whole worship team to help with props and costumes can be a playful way to build camaraderie; it's also a good way to be sure that actors are physically comfortable in their roles. For example, the service called "Strong Is What We Make Each Other" features two main characters: Hare and Monkey. How do your actors imagine bringing those beings to life? Does the person playing Hare feel comfortable wearing rabbit ears and a cotton tail pinned to his seat, or would your actor prefer to use a puppet?

From one month before the service until the rehearsal itself, trust that your team's brainstorming will result in "aha" moments. I'm continually surprised by the treasures that lurk in my parishioners' closets and attics ("I have some plastic armor and swords at home. Wouldn't that be great for the soldiers?" "Yes, and I have some pink cowboy boots that you could wear."). Common sense should rule here: your actors still need to be able to move, for example. And stairs don't mix well with masks that limit vision. You'll also want to remind each other to label the props and costume pieces that are entrusted to you, so they don't end up in a lost-and-found bin forever.

While a well-placed prop or a vivid costume piece can add visual sizzle to a service, try not to become overly concerned with flashy presentation. It's enough for each character to have just one costume piece or prop—whether it's a crown, a cape, or a cooking pot—to create a sense of fun and stimulate imaginations.

Consider Each Liturgical Element

Worship for all ages gives you and your team the opportunity to take a fresh look at each of the elements of worship. This may mean change, which can add zest, making new space for the movement of the Spirit. But change can also create anxiety by removing familiar "mileposts" that mark the course of the service. I encourage you not to take any element for granted, but rather to consider each of the following individually and make intentional decisions about how that element can best serve the whole worship experience.

Prelude/Gathering Music. Many congregations begin their services with some form of gathering or centering music. The language of song is as important as the words we speak, so work with your music professionals to select pieces that will complement the theme of your service.

Welcome and Greeting. The first address to the congregation can set a tone for the entire service. If you'd like to go beyond the spoken welcome, consider a more interactive, playful option—for example, two worship leaders can demonstrate a gesture or sign to accompany a verbal greeting. They might say "Good morning" while patting their heads and shaking hands or bowing low to one another. They might even greet one another in a different language, perhaps sign language. Then congregation members can be invited to turn and greet their neighbors in the same way.

Chalice Lighting. In some churches, the congregation recites a brief reading in unison as the chalice is lit. In others, the chalice is lit in silence, or while the Leader offers words. Other congregations invite an entire family to process down the center aisle and a child from the family ceremonially lights the chalice.

Some congregations like to incorporate movement into the chalice lighting by using some form of the words that follow. Once the congregation learns this chalice lighting, a volunteer can come forward to act out the corresponding movements as the chalice is lit:

We light this chalice

[*holds up arms, forearms together with palms upturned*]

. . . symbol of Unitarian Universalism

[*makes a U on each hand with the thumb and index finger*]

We are the [church/home] of the open mind

[*places fingertips on forehead, and moves hands out into the air*]

We are the [church/home] of the helping hands

[*holds hands out, palms up*]

We are the [church/home] of the loving hearts.

[*crosses arms across heart*]

Sharing Joys and Sorrows. Every congregation seems to have a different level of affection (or aversion) for sharing joys and sorrows, also known as "joys and concerns" or "milestones." Almost no other subject in a Unitarian Universalist congregation can raise passions as quickly as a debate about the value of this ritual. In this book, I've made the bold assumption that your congregation and its leadership have found a comfortable and responsible way to share joys and sorrows—but, as with any other liturgical element, it can be removed at your discretion. If you choose to include it, and if yours is a congregation where the sharing of joys and sorrows is an exercise in patience, keep in mind that children may become restless after more than a few minutes.

Silence. In these services, the sharing of joys and sorrows is followed by a moment of silent meditation. It's remarkable how brief this time is in some congregations—blink, and it's over! Perhaps we've forgotten that the point isn't so much to achieve silence as it is to experience *being* among the rustling, breathing, and shifting around us. It's a chance to let our spirits catch up with our bodies and notice what's happening in our hearts.

Allow at least a full minute to go by. Remember: Everything we do is a way of teaching children. Ending the silent meditation after ten seconds teaches people not to get too comfortable with themselves in the unfolding of time. Lingering in quietude, on the other hand, teaches our children—and adults—how to practice being comfortable in stillness.

Offering. When we speak mindfully of the offering and intentionally circulate the plates or baskets, we communicate something to those present about the stewardship of our congregations. If you're looking for a way to playfully introduce change and to include young ones, you might use silly hats as offering receptacles. Rather than circulating them during the service, take a moment at the beginning of worship to request two or three volunteers. Give the volunteers the hats and let the congregation know that they will stand at the door at the end of the service to collect the offering as people leave.

Several of these scripts offer an opportunity to share in non-monetary stewardship during the service, such as a food offering of canned goods for a local organization. (When planning such an offering, it may be useful to coordinate with your social justice or outreach committee.) An offering of canned goods provides a great opportunity for worshipers to move their bodies by bringing their offering forward. Adults with limited mobility can give theirs to children, who often enjoy being couriers.

Rehearse

As you recruit volunteers and give them the worship script, ask them to commit to attending a rehearsal. If you're including children or youth, it's best to check in with them as individuals, as well as with their parents. As a general rule, rehearsals are most effective when they're held a week or less before the service. Usually the more people you involve in a service, the more time you'll need to sort out who goes where and when. So, depending on the number of actors and musicians, your rehearsal could last between one and three hours. Rehearsal is not optional; it's as important as the service itself. Not all roles need to be rehearsed—the list of roles for each service indicates those that do.

These rehearsals are exercises in controlled chaos. Begin by making sure that everyone knows one another; perhaps even do an ice-breaking activity together. Then run through the service several times so that people feel comfortable with the script, props, movements, and timing. (It can take a few run-throughs just to learn when and how to enter and leave.) The rehearsal is a great opportunity to brainstorm ways to flesh out the story or iron out trouble spots.

The rehearsal is also a good time for all involved to get in touch with their inner silly selves. Invite each person's voice to emerge and come through. If you have a perfectionist side, or if someone on your team does, it's important to remind everyone that creating and leading worship is as much about relationships as it is about "the performance." Use the rehearsal as a chance to find new gifts in people, and be guided by the line from Ric Masten's hymn "Let It Be a Dance": "If nothing's wrong, then nothing's right."

You can also reduce stress by telling your actors not to memorize their lines. Professional entertainment is not the goal of multigenerational worship, and the service will be more authentic and enjoyable if your actors are relaxed and at ease, with their scripts in front of them. Not having to remember lines frees actors to spontaneously embody what they are reading. Encourage your actors to print their lines in a large font, if helpful, or in any other customized way that will make their reading easier.

Along with giving ourselves permission to make mistakes and to read from the script, there's one more note of grace that actors and musicians should keep in mind: The service isn't a job to plow through as quickly as possible. Your team should take its time telling these stories and let the nonverbal parts of the service play themselves out.

I sometimes think of worship (perhaps irreverently) as planning a party with Spirit, and then inviting the entire congregation to join in. As you act out the story in a worship setting, you will also be *in relationship* with the congregation—everyone from the five-year-olds to the ninety-five-year-olds. When the congregation laughs, let the laughter play itself out before taking up the script again. If someone doesn't complete his action on cue, wait for him to catch up (and ad-lib: "It was a longer journey than he expected. Yup: a veeeeerrrrry long journey.") If there's a glitch that seems to stall the service, don't panic. Nobody watching knows exactly what's supposed to happen—and besides, people will be as forgiving of mistakes as you are towards each other.

Tips on Interactive Worship

If bringing these services to life means being in relationship with the congregation, that means that *they* will be in relationship with *you*—the actors, readers, and musicians. Our churches are filled with good-hearted people who want you to succeed and will step into the spaces that you create for them. That's good, because a common element in these services is the opportunity for people to share their responses to something in the service. The Leader or the Storyteller is usually charged with managing these responses, which demands some on-the-spot processing.

It's essential to voice a gentle expectation that people will raise their hands if they wish to share. Otherwise, the bolder, more extroverted members of your congregation will dominate these intervals, and children may absorb the implicit message that shouting out in worship is okay.

While it's nice to call on people by name, it would be even nicer to think that our congregations are so thriving and so full of newcomers that we can't possibly know everyone's name! Don't avoid calling on someone simply because you don't know them. It's acceptable to point directly to a raised hand and invite a response. Be sure to call upon children and youth, as well as adults.

When someone gives a response, always repeat into the microphone a summary of what was just said. That way, everyone can hear what's going on. You're likely to discover that adult and child responses complement each other quite well. Predictably, children provide more concrete responses to questions, while adult offerings are more abstract and nuanced. Summarizing and repeating responses allows you to reframe them as they roll in and to draw connections between them.

You can allow these responses to unfold at their own pace—but you should also feel comfortable limiting them. You don't need to call upon all who raise their hands. Sometimes only a few responses are needed to pull the service into the next stage.

A final note about the impulse to express joy collectively: Congregations vary widely in their level of comfort with applause during worship. Some churches want to show appreciation for those whose talents bring us delight or move us to new depths, and feel that applause is the best way to do that. Others believe that applause can disrupt a tone of reverence or can lead congregants to feel obligated to applaud every person who speaks or sings. One way to channel applause energy in the service is to introduce it in its sign language form: hands in the air, palms facing front, fingers wiggling. Don't be afraid to experiment!

Borrowing from Other Cultures

Nearly all of these worship services are grounded in story. Whether it's a story as old as the Nativity or as modern as Carl Sagan's reflections on a picture of Earth taken from outer space, our minds and hearts are awakened by any form of the phrase "Once upon a time . . ."

When the story comes from the folk tradition of another culture, the script contains some words to frame it within its original context. It's important to convey the story's cultural context and significance—or even *elaborate* on it if someone from that culture can be involved in the service. For example, if you have a volunteer of Chinese descent, she might provide a rich explanation of what makes "Good News, Bad News" a Chinese wisdom story. Or if one of your volunteers has a Jewish background, he might be included in the service titled "The Right Way to Right Speech" by helping to explain Yiddish—or even offering a spontaneous demonstration. (A gentle caution: before you reach out, be clear about the distinction between *inviting* people to elaborate on their tradition and *pressuring* them into being spokespeople or interpreters for their culture.)

Providing cultural context is a way to make visible our Unitarian Universalist commitment to right relationship—not just our relationships with each other but also with the cultures and peoples whose stories, words, and ideas we incorporate into our worship. At one level, of course, there's the relationship of us all being part of one human family. At another level, there may be a relationship of oppressor and oppressed. There may even be still other levels. Be mindful to present stories, songs, and rituals in ways that do justice to these multiple levels of relationship. Addressing the question "Who are the people whose story we are hearing?" helps to imbue that relationship with respect, rather than with a sense of proprietorship.

Of course, it takes much more than a script to effect a cultural shift in congregational worship style. In these pages, I hope you'll find interesting ideas, laughter, and fun vehicles for honoring liberal religious values. But all of these services are like seeds: They will take root and bloom only if there is fertile soil to receive them. Worship becomes exciting and transformational only if the congregation invites it to be so. It is true that the congregations I've served have been changed and enriched by these services. It's just as true that those transformations were made possible by those congregations' eagerness to be together for a full hour on Sunday mornings as communities of all ages, rather than just for the first ten or fifteen minutes of every service. The congregations that get the most out of these services are also those that encourage experimentation with new forms of worship in order to find out what works, what touches hearts and souls, and what doesn't. They value risk-taking and understand that risk is implicit in growth. They participate good-naturedly in new or experimental worship services and accept with grace the inevitable growing edges that present themselves in any trial-and-error process. They understand the value of learning by doing.

In other words, vibrant and exciting multigenerational worship flourishes when congregations and their leaders whole-heartedly embrace their call to serve *all* of their members; it happens when they empower worship leaders to venture into uncharted territory, and ready themselves to receive the fruits of those labors with humor and acceptance. May your congregation be one of them.

What Will You Bring to the Feast?
Start of the Church Year

This folk tale about trickery at a royal feast is based on the story "Water Not Wine," based on African and Chinese folk tales and retold by Elisa Davy Pearmain. It provides a fresh lens for our Unitarian Universalist tradition of the water ceremony, also called "water communion," "ingathering," or "homecoming." As we begin a new congregational year by mingling our various contributions of water from the summer, each of us must answer these questions: Will I contribute the best of myself to this beloved community? Will I share my gifts, adding to our abundance, or will I hold back my gifts for my own use?

Preparation (minimal)

- Publicize the fact that this service includes an offering of canned goods for a local food bank.

- Ask the congregation to bring water collected during the summer to the service.

- Gather 10 pitchers or vases, assigning each to a Council Member. (These remain under their seats until the banquet scene.) In addition, each Council Member, the Village Elder, and the Wife should have a cup or glass for the banquet scene.

- Have the words to "How Our Garden Grows" printed in the order of service.

- Reserve the first few rows of one section of the sanctuary for the Council Members.

- Place a large bowl in a prominent place on the altar, the chancel, or a central table; this may be the same bowl you use for the water ceremony in the second half of the service. Put a pitcher of water beside it for those who may not have brought water with them.
- Assign one Council Member to speak the line of dialogue attributed to "Any Council Member."
- *Rehearsal will take about 1 hour.*

Roles (14, those who need to attend rehearsal are marked with *)

- Storyteller*
- Leader*
- Village Elder*
- Youngest Council Member*
- Youngest Council Member's Wife* (called "Wife" in script)
- 9 additional Council Members

As the service begins, the Storyteller and the Leader are at the front of the sanctuary. The Village Elder and Council Members are seated in the first few rows of seats. The bowl and pitcher are in place on the altar or a table.

STORYTELLER Imagine. Imagine a land far from this one, and a time much different from our own. Imagine that you are the village elder, who owns many fields and stables full of livestock. Imagine that your harvest this year has been the most successful ever, and that you're grateful to the Powers That Be in the universe for this bounty. What would you do to celebrate? How would you express your gratitude? [*invites suggestions from the congregation*]

Those are wonderful ideas, each with its own story. In the story you'll hear and see this morning, an ancient tale with roots in Africa and China, this village elder will have his own idea about how to celebrate.

Village Elder stands to greet the congregation.

You'll meet the council members of his village, and you'll hear how they taught their village an embarrassing and important lesson. What could it be? We'll find out soon after our worship begins.
The Leader thanks the Storyteller. Village Elder sits.

Welcome

The Leader welcomes congregants and visitors.

LEADER Now that we've greeted each other, we enter into our annual ingathering service: We symbolize our coming together after a summer of traveling and rest; we celebrate all that is life-giving and that which has restored our spirits. Our water ceremony today is a visible sign that, no matter where we go and for how long, our love of this community—and the love from this community—draws us back in, warm and welcoming. May we also consider what we bring to this community on the cusp of a new year together.

Chalice Lighting

"Love Will Guide Us," *SLT,* 131

Village Elder stands before the congregation.

STORYTELLER Let's return to our story. In that land far away, in that time so different from ours, it had been a glorious harvest year for the village elder, the richest person in the valley. He was grateful for his many fields of grain, and for his stables full of livestock. As an expression of gratitude, he decided to share his riches with all the people of his valley: He would hold a feast for all his neighbors! But the elder needed help with one aspect of the feast. To get that help, and to issue the invitation to the feast, he called together the ten members of the village council.

Council Members stand up from their seats in the congregation or lean forward and listen as Village Elder approaches them.

VILLAGE ELDER I have had a great harvest this year, and my stables are full of livestock. There's much to be thankful for, and so I shall hold a great feast for all the people of this valley. I will provide all the food; I will provide musicians and jugglers; I will provide the space for this feast. I will do all of this, if you will provide the wine.

COUNCIL MEMBERS Of course, of course!

ANY MEMBER We shall each bring one jug of wine, and pour them into a common vessel. Thus shall we share, even as we partake of your generosity.

STORYTELLER With that, the council members returned to their homes, dreaming of the great feast to come.

Village Elder and Council Members take seats.

LEADER Just as the village elder responded to the abundance of his harvest with gratitude and giving, so too do we recognize, and give thanks for, all the blessings in our lives. Like the village elder, many of us have more food than other members of our wider community, and so we share our abundance of food with them. Please bring forward your canned goods or give them to a child to bring forward for the food offering as we sing "From You I Receive."

"From You I Receive," *SLT,* 402

STORYTELLER The village elder had just announced his plans to hold a great feast. Before returning to their homes, each of the council members in the village had agreed to bring one jug of wine to contribute to the common pot. As soon as they parted, however, the youngest was already cursing himself for having agreed to part with a whole jug of wine. He didn't have much wine in his stores, and he didn't want to spend money. He returned to his wife, and told her what he had agreed to. She shared his misgivings.

Youngest Council Member and his Wife take center stage.

YOUNGEST COUNCIL MEMBER   An entire jug of wine? Are we to give up so much, when we don't have as much as others? There must be another way.

STORYTELLER   Suddenly his wife had an idea.

WIFE   My dear, the other nine council members will pour their wine into the common pot. Is that not so? Could one small jug of water really spoil so much wine?

YOUNGEST COUNCIL MEMBER   Hardly so, my clever wife! What a plan! Thus will we keep our wine for ourselves!

The couple exits. Village Elder and Council Members return.

STORYTELLER   While the youngest council member and his wife were crafting their plan, the people in the valley received their invitation to the feast with great anticipation. Finally, the evening of the feast arrived. As the villagers dressed in their finest clothes, so did the youngest council member—and then, as planned, he surreptitiously filled his jug with fresh water from the well. He and his wife carried their jug to the party, meeting the other council members and all the townspeople along the way. When they arrived at the estate of the village elder, everyone was greeted by the sound of music playing and the delicious smells of food cooking.

VILLAGE ELDER   Welcome to this great feast! Thank you for bringing your wine. You may pour your jugs of wine into that great clay pot in the courtyard, and then take your fill of food.

Council Members come forward one at a time and pantomime pouring the wine from their pitchers and vases into the bowl.

STORYTELLER   And so the village council members, including the youngest, all emptied their jugs into the common pot and made ready for the feast. And what a feast it was! First there was dancing and entertainment. Then the bell was rung and the guests were seated. The council members gathered together at the head table. Everyone's cup had been filled, and everyone was anxious to taste the fine, refreshing wine.

Council Members gather, standing, in semi-circle around Village Elder, while Wife sits in front row. All of them pull out their cups or glasses.

VILLAGE ELDER   Before we share this meal and drink this wine, let us give thanks: We give thanks for the work of the earth and sun, as they have ripened the fruits of the earth to fill our bellies. We give thanks for the hands that have prepared this food, so that we might eat it. We give thanks for the company gathered here—all those who make our village a place of abundance, especially by bringing their gifts to share with us in generosity.

LEADER   We, too, pause to give thanks—for our summer, no matter how we filled its days: working or resting; playing or seeking adventure; finding new pleasures at home or exploring new corners of the world. We give thanks that we safely found our way here this morning. We give thanks for this congregation, and all those in it: those with a welcoming spirit, those with a questioning mind, those with embracing arms, those with a prophet's vision. Let us sing our thanks, as we turn to hymn 1010, "We Give Thanks."

"We Give Thanks," *STJ,* 1010

Council Members and Village Elder remain standing, with their cups, as the hymn is sung. They then act out the following scene as it is described.

STORYTELLER   The crowd had gathered, the food had been served, thanks had been given. Finally, it was time to eat! After the village elder's blessing, every guest at the feast lifted his or her cup, and then brought the cup to their lips. They sipped, and sipped again. But something was wrong. What they tasted was not wine, but water.

YOUNGEST COUNCIL MEMBER   [*steps forward to address Wife in a stage whisper*] "One jug of water cannot spoil a great pot of wine." So we told ourselves, and so we filled our jug at the well. But clearly, every council member had the same thought! They all filled their jugs at the well! And so instead of sharing our wine to suit this great occasion, we have done nothing but embarrass ourselves.

STORYTELLER   All the council members looked at each other sheepishly, avoiding the eyes of the village elder, and then continued to drink as if it were the finest wine they had ever tasted. The next day a new saying arose among the people of the town, a saying that spread around the world: "If you wish to take wine, you must give it also."

The actors return to their seats, with thanks.

LEADER   As we reflect on this story and its lesson, please join me in the sung response, "How Our Garden Grows," printed in your order of service.

The following words are sung to the melody "Cranham," by Gustav Holst, SLT, *241.*

"How Our Garden Grows"
How our garden grows; how we harvest love:
We plant seeds that blossom; the fruit grows forth thereof.
How our garden grows: with stewardship and care.
Hearts and souls become strong from our gifts freely shared.

LEADER   Wisdom can arise independently, and often does, in different parts of the world. The story we just heard has been told by cultures in both Africa and China. Similar stories are also told by people in different lands—which is the human family's way of signaling that the story contains an important universal truth. Hearing this story today, we can appreciate its truth, too: When we share with our community, it is truly felt and appreciated; but when we try to withhold from our community and keep something all to ourselves, it can hurt the community. Do you remember what the council members in our story were asked to bring to the feast? [*allows someone to say "wine"*]

Unlike them, you were asked to bring water to this worship service. If you didn't remember, you can use the water here in this pitcher. This is our [Ingathering/Homecoming/Water Communion] Sunday: the time when we merge our various portions of waters from the summer. Traditionally, this ritual is celebrated by many Unitarian Universalist congregations across the country by people bringing forward their water and naming its source, or what that water represents. Today, our water ceremony will diverge from that tradition in a small but significant way: We're thankful for all of you who experienced the joy of learning about a new place in the world, or who revisited a familiar and well-loved place, over the summer. We're thankful that as you traveled by car, airplane, boat, train, and trolley those travels brought you home safely. We also recognize that not everyone has the resources, or the ability, to travel to faraway lands. Although it's interesting to hear where people have traveled in past weeks, that practice is a looking back and a looking outward. Our water ceremony today calls us to a higher purpose: that of looking forward, and committing ourselves to the common life of this congregation—just as our individual samples of water combine in this common vessel.

It is important to consider how we each contribute to the larger community, making it stronger, more peaceful, and more friendly. In our story this morning, the ten council members were asked to bring a small amount of wine to the feast. As you heard, each of them withheld their wine, and instead brought water, believing that the lack of one jug of wine could hardly spoil such a lavish feast. From that story, we learned the importance of each person's gifts, and each person's willingness to share those gifts. What is it that you bring to our community? What will you share, from your heart and your spirit, in the coming year? These are the questions at the heart of our water ceremony.

I invite you to come forward, row by row, as individuals or families, and form lines at the common vessel. When you pour your water in, please name one gift that you bring to our new congregational year. Perhaps it's a desire to attend worship more regularly, or to listen to others more carefully. Maybe you bring the gift of patience (always valuable, especially in committee meetings). Maybe you bring a musical talent that you're willing to share, or a commitment to teach religious education. Let's take a minute or two to reflect. Parents, take a moment to talk with your families about what gifts you each bring to this congregation, or to the larger community. Then, as you pour in your water, tell us the gifts that you bring, that you're willing to share with others.

The Leader waits a minute or two for people to frame their thoughts, then gestures people forward and waits in silence during the sharing. If the congregation is too large for individual sharing, or if the open mic format is inappropriate, the Council Members' ten pitchers may be passed up and down the aisles for people to pour their water into. They can speak of their gifts to the people next to them.

Here, mingled together, are the shared gifts of our lives. These waters represent the promises and aspirations that we make with one another, members of this beloved community. As we enter into a space of quiet, let us consider the part of ourselves that fears giving out love freely. In this quiet, let us resolve not to withhold our love, but to follow love's path and its progress wherever it leads.

Source of All, who embraces and sustains all life,
this water, which we have collected and shared,
holds the mystery and miracle of love.
May this water be blessed with the love of this community.
May our own bodies, filled with rivers of breath,
be blessed with life-energy, with wellness,
to carry us through our days.
May our home, this blue-green planet,
with its mountains and seas and ice caps,
be held in sacred keeping,
blessed through our stewardship and care.
As we strive to bring our gifts to this beloved community
and to this difficult, beautiful world,
let us never doubt the strength of our hearts,
nor the depth of our love for each other and our world.

"Blue Boat Home," *STJ,* 1064

LEADER We take an offering each Sunday, to give of our material resources with generosity and gratitude. No matter how much money you put into the basket, the act of giving is a symbolic reminder that giving is just as important as receiving; that sharing what we have is how we live out our value of generosity.

Offering

"Now Let Us Sing," *SLT,* 368

LEADER Sing to the power of the faith within—
Sing to the power of our deep love,
Our strong hope, and bright joy.
But flex the power of these gifts, too—
put your faith and hope to use;
share your joy and love more freely than you thought possible,
for together, we use these tools to carve out
lives of wonder, and purpose, and service.

Go in peace.

Following Yonder Star
Christmas

Many of us sing the carol "We Three Kings" at the holidays—but who were the three kings, the magi? This service, which works well as an alternative holiday pageant or Christmas Eve service, playfully explores the legend of the magi, reimagining the story to include their wives, who also make the journey to Bethlehem. The story invites listeners to reflect on what calls us forward on our own journeys.

Preparation (moderate)

- Gather a scroll of paper (Caspar's star chart); a telescope or kaleidoscope that can be easily carried; traveling bundles; a cooking pot and spoon; shears and fabric; ornate boxes for gold, frankincense, and myrrh; a baby Jesus in his manger; at least 1 camel cutout or puppet, or as many as 6 of them; pretty pillows; and a shawl and/or blanket.
- Reserve 3 places in the front row of seats for Azadeh, Lilya, and Tehmina.
- *Rehearsal will take between 2 and 3 hours.*

Roles (11–16, those who need to attend rehearsal are marked with *)

- Leader*
- Caspar*
- Melchior*
- Balthazar*

- Azadeh* (ah-ZAH-deh), Caspar's wife
- Lilya*, Melchior's wife
- Tehmina* (teh-MEEN-ah), Balthazar's wife
- Mary
- Joseph
- Reader
- Camel* (non-speaking role; manipulates camel cutout or puppet)
- *optional*: 5 additional Camels* (also non-speaking)

As the service begins, Caspar and Azadeh are at the front of the sanctuary. Caspar has his telescope in hand and is completely engrossed in his star chart and talking to himself as if in a reverie.

CASPAR How strange. [*pauses*] Very strange. [*pauses*] How very, very strange. [*pauses*] Very, very, very, very, very, ver—

AZADEH What is so very strange, Caspar?

CASPAR No time to explain, my dear—I must find Melchior and Balthazar. They need to know what I saw in last night's sky ... although I still can't account for it. Ah—there's Melchior now! Excuse me.

Caspar rushes down the aisle with his telescope and star chart, just as Melchior comes up the aisle toward him. The two meet and pantomime an animated conversation, examining the star chart as they talk, while Azadeh delivers her lines.

AZADEH [*to congregation*] I know that look in his eye: There's a mysterious sign to be interpreted. My husband, Caspar, watches the skies every night, tracking the star patterns as they move from season to season. That's Melchior he's speaking with; he, too, reads the stars. For them, the stars' patterns are messages from the cosmos about events yet to happen.

Balthazar joins Caspar and Melchior in the aisle; the three continue to talk silently as Azadeh continues.

That third man is another friend, Balthazar. He frequently comes to our house on some pretense or other, and stays to take the evening meal with us. Balthazar is a healer. He prepares salves and tonics to treat bodily illness, but he also listens to people's dreams, interpreting them and offering guidance for troubled souls. Oh, forgive me—I didn't introduce myself. My name is Azadeh, meaning "free one." My parents named me wisely, for I've always had the strength to make decisions and take actions with confidence.

The three men exit the sanctuary.

There go the men. Some great plan is no doubt afoot. If you'll excuse me, I need to find the wives of Melchior and Balthazar. I wonder if Lilya and Tehmina have any idea why our husbands are so agitated. [*exits*]

Welcome

The Leader enters and welcomes congregants and visitors.

LEADER   We're worshiping together this morning as we tell an ancient story in a new way. In doing so, we celebrate that our congregation spans many decades of life, a range of religious beliefs, and a depth of life experiences. We celebrate the differences that provide our liberal religious community with rich texture, and we celebrate that which unites us: a choice to be guided by love and respect. Did any of the names we just heard—Caspar, Melchior, and Balthazar—sound familiar to any of you? [*allows congregation to offer comments*]

Caspar, Melchior, and Balthazar are the names that the Western Christian tradition, in the eighth century, gave to the wise men, or magi, who came to visit the baby Jesus just a few days after his birth. No one knows what their names really were, but the magi were likely priests of an ancient Indo-Iranian religion called Zoroastrianism. During Roman times, when Jesus lived, these priests were recognized as physician-astrologers who healed the sick, interpreted dreams, and cast horoscopes. They were considered to be "wise men"—very knowledgeable about the world around them, and just as knowledgeable about the stars. What do you know about the wise men? [*invites a few quick responses*]

It's hard to know what's really true about the magi. Two of the four gospels in the New Testament tell the story of Jesus' birth. Only one of them, the Gospel according to Matthew, mentions the magi visiting the stable in Bethlehem. Since these figures are a part of the Christmas story, this morning we're going to imagine the story behind the story, from an entirely new angle. Let's begin with a couple of things that may be familiar to us: lighting the chalice, and then singing "O Little Town of Bethlehem."

Chalice Lighting

"O Little Town of Bethlehem," *SLT,* 246

Azadeh, Lilya, and Tehmina come forward.

LILYA   My husband has been talking in hushed tones with Caspar and Balthazar all morning. I wonder what signs they've seen.

AZADEH   The stars foretell something significant. Caspar hardly slept after reading the sky last night.

TEHMINA   Some great event must be making itself known through dreams as well, for Balthazar slept little. Instead, he paced the floor for many hours—he always does that when he's divining the message in a dream.

LILYA   Here they come! Surely they'll be too preoccupied to tell us of their thoughts.

TEHMINA   I want to know their plans; all three of us do. The meaning of my name, Tehmina, is "strong woman," and indeed I am strong—stubborn, too. Sisters, let's hide ourselves and see whether we can overhear their conversation.

The women hide from the men, staying within view of the congregation. The men walk up the aisle to take center stage and have the following conversation as the women silently react.

CASPAR   As we have told you, Balthazar, our studies of the night sky convince us that the birth of an important baby is imminent.

BALTHAZAR   I know less of stars than I do of dreams, gentlemen, and I had a powerful dream last night. There was a long road leading to a simple building, which glowed with a golden aura. Inside the walls, I could hear the cries of an infant. The crying gave way to heavenly song, as if the angels themselves were singing. I awoke from the dream with the conviction that such a scene will unfold, and that I must make a journey to that place.

MELCHIOR   [*in wonder*] I, too, feel that the stars have been calling me. We're being summoned. We must find this child.

BALTHAZAR   But where? In what direction do the stars point?

CASPAR   Far to the west, we think, nearly to the sea; possibly the hills of Judea. It would be a journey of many days.

MELCHIOR   Westward we'll go. And who is this child, do you suppose?

CASPAR   Given the remarkable arrangement of stars, he's likely a king: a baby who will grow up to be a ruler of nations.

BALTHAZAR   It could just as easily be a healer we seek, a child who will grow up with miraculous powers to make the sick well.

MELCHIOR   But Balthazar, if you saw a golden aura and heard angels in your dream, the babe we seek may be a holy person, who can speak to the gods.

CASPAR   Friends, we do not need the answer to that question at this moment. We need only decide whether to follow the star signs to the child, and how soon to leave.

MELCHIOR   . . . and what to tell our wives, of course. They won't like us making such a long journey, and they'll want to go with us.

BALTHAZAR   They can come with us, as long as we don't allow Tehmina to do the cooking.

Tehmina, from her hiding place, reacts.

CASPAR How can they come with us? And why would they? There is no need for them to visit this child. Let us go alone, my brothers, and let us prepare now. We'll take rest during this afternoon's hot sun, and take our leave at dusk. The camels will carry us through each night as we follow the star signs.

MELCHIOR Agreed. Let us prepare our things—and let us include gifts to take to this important baby, whoever he or she is. We must arrive with generous tokens of honor and esteem.

CASPAR You're right, Melchior. If the baby is a king in the making, the proper gift would be gold. I shall visit the temple today, and select a piece of gold to carry with us.

BALTHAZAR We don't know that the child is a ruler, Caspar. I have proposed that he or she might be a healer, in which case we ought to present ointment and anointing oil made with myrrh. I will prepare some jars immediately.

MELCHIOR Friends, you both forget that the babe could be a holy person. The only fitting gift would be the finest incense—frankincense—to perfume his robes and hair.

CASPAR Since we disagree, let us each take our own gift. But let us make our preparations now, so that the journey can begin tonight.

The men exit; the women, still upset at what they've overheard, leave their hiding place and come forward and sit in the front row.

LEADER It's an ancient story, and a familiar one: Whether wise healers or ordinary people, sometimes we're called forward into a new journey. Many of us here know what it's like to be summoned beyond ourselves. We arrive at a crossroads, with possibility laid out before us, and within us. Amid uncertainty, sometimes it's possible to receive fragments of guidance: a dream calls to us; a random turn of fate feels like a "sign"; the voice of wisdom makes itself known to us. This is joy: to feel safe and confident as our lives unfold in ways that feel right, to take a path that rewards us. Our journeys can also lead to sorrow. When our hopes don't come to pass; when the world's randomness seems to seek us out for ruin; when even our most careful decisions turn out to feel punishing—at these times, we need to be reminded of life's goodness, and the strength that others may lend us. During this time of sharing our joys and sorrows, let us make room for this full breadth of our experiences: the tragedies, the sweet celebrations, and everything in between.

Joys and Sorrows

After the congregation has shared, the Leader calls for a period of silent meditation and allows at least a minute of silence.

"The Hills Are Bare at Bethlehem," *SLT,* 232

Azadeh, Lilya, and Tehmina take center stage.

LILYA   Travel without us? So far to the west? How many days will they sleep in the harsh desert, unguarded and vulnerable?

TEHMINA   I don't care if he has to eat sand at every meal.

AZADEH   Balthazar meant no harm, Tehmina. And Lilya, our husbands can take care of each other.

LILYA   That's true.

AZADEH   My friends, what do you think of our husbands' other plan? If this star does herald a majestic birth, there will be a baby, a new family in need of care—and yet our husbands speak of carrying gold, frankincense, and myrrh.

LILYA   What infant needs such empty extravagance? There will be a mother needing rest and a father to be fed. Sweet-smelling incense will mean little after a few nights without sleep. I hope this child's parents receive visitors who will care for them, rather than bestow useless gifts on the baby.

AZADEH   [*slowly*] We could. We could be those visitors.

TEHMINA We could follow our husbands, as they follow the stars.

AZADEH Of course! We're no strangers to the desert, and we have our own strong camels. We'll disguise ourselves as men, and bring our own gifts to this heralded baby.

LILYA I like your idea, Azadeh. I was given the name Lilya, or "dark night," because I was born in starlight. I've always wanted to travel under the cloak of stars. Let's go! Although Melchior brings frankincense to honor the birth of a holy person, I will bring something that smells just as delicious: my finest cooking pot, and herbs, to cook rich stews for the babe's mother.

TEHMINA And my husband brings myrrh to honor the birth of a healer. I don't have my husband's healing abilities, but I know how to help a body be at rest. I shall bring a gift of sheep shears and the finest fabrics. I'll create soft pillows for the family, and will weave delicate bunting for the babe.

AZADEH Caspar brings gold because he believes the child to be a king-in-the-making. I have nothing so fine in my possession, but I do have the gift of singing. I shall sit by the baby's side, singing her to sleep with gentle melodies.

All three men, and Lilya and Tehmina, act out the following scene as Azadeh describes it. If the service includes one Camel, it stays with the women, leading them out when they leave. If there are six Camels, each traveler follows a Camel as they move, effecting a trot and making galloping noises.

AZADEH [*stepping forward to address the congregation*] And so our secret journey began. We cheerfully helped each of our husbands prepare a bundle of supplies. Into Caspar's went a nugget of gold. Melchior tucked generous amounts of frankincense into his bag, and Balthazar's bundle contained jars of myrrh. We watched them load their camels at twilight, and they struck out on their journey westward. [*allows time for the goodbyes and men's departure, before continuing*] As soon as they'd left, we women packed for our own journey. Tehmina's camel carried thick rolls of the softest cottons and silks, wrapped around her sheep shears. Inside Lilya's bundle, the round sides of a cooking pot were visible. Since my voice takes up no space, I loaded food and a tent onto my camel. With our husbands still visible on the horizon—thanks to the light of the moon—we set out behind them in a silent caravan.

The women exit the sanctuary with Camel(s).

LEADER   What gifts do we bring to this community—gifts we might share within these walls and beyond them? How little would it take from each of us to form a significant gift that might make a big difference? As we contribute to the offering, our ritual of stewardship, let us give of ourselves to the larger whole: not because there isn't need somewhere else, nor because we are a perfect community. Rather, let us share our gifts this morning out of gratitude for all that we have, in trust that our offering will find its way to grateful recipients.

Offering

LEADER   Jubilate [*you-bih-LAH-tay*] is a song of joy and thanks. Remembering the wise men and wise women—and wise children—everywhere who have set out on journeys of faith and courage, let us sing our next hymn, voicing our "Jubilate."

"Now on Land and Sea Descending," *SLT,* 47

LEADER   [*prayerfully*] Like the magi and the women in this story, maybe you have set out on an uncertain journey at some time in your life. What was it like to be carried forward? Perhaps you were unsure where the journey would take you, or whether you would be strong enough to keep going. Maybe your journey led you through delightful twists, or delivered you somewhere you never expected to end up. May we reflect, for these few moments, on all the journeys that began in hope, and in which our hope was rewarded. Take some time to count the forks in the road that, once taken, led to happy discoveries and to meaningful relationships.

Know your courage and strength, which you have shown in making those journeys.

Remember the moments of "peace profound" that came to you when the path seemed particularly risky. Ask yourself, silently, what guided you forward. Recall the ways you have experienced "the Care that cares for all" moving through your life, guiding you just as the stars led the magi to that stable in Bethlehem. How does "the Care that cares for all" continue to express itself in your life?

May we rest in the confidence of changeless love:
The Holy's love for each of us;
Our love for one another, as members of a beloved community;
The love that has held us to our journeys, and carries us forward.

Mary and Joseph, with the baby Jesus in the manger, take center stage and sit, acting out the following scenes as they are narrated.

It is told in the Gospel according to Luke: While Mary and Joseph were there in Bethlehem, the time came for the baby to be born, and she gave birth to her firstborn, a son. She wrapped him in cloths and placed him in a manger, because there was no room for them in the inn. And there were shepherds living out in the fields nearby, keeping watch over their flocks at night. An angel of the Lord appeared to them, and the glory of the Lord shone around them, and they were terrified. But the angel said to them, "Do not be afraid. I bring you good news of great joy that will be for all the people. Today in the town of David a Savior has been born to you; he is Christ the Lord. This will be a sign to you: you will find a baby wrapped in cloths and lying in a manger." And so the cries of the infant became a heavenly host of voices, singing. Thus it was that the magi appeared at the stable, offering their gifts.

Let us sing together "We Three Kings."

As the congregation sings the first verse, the magi and their Camels approach the seated family (they may be singing along with the congregation). On the second verse, Melchior makes a show of his gift of frankincense to the family; there's time for him to lift the box/bag, to bow before the manger, etc. Balthazar does the same on the third verse, presenting myrrh, and Caspar presents his gift of gold on the fourth and final verse.

"We Three Kings of Orient Are," *SLT,* 259

After the hymn, the magi continue to gaze at the baby.

CASPAR   Great things will become of this child.

MELCHIOR   May he live long, and know peace for all his days.

BALTHAZAR   [*to the baby*] I hope you like the gifts.

The men slowly walk down the aisle, exiting the sanctuary, as the Reader steps forward. If each man has his own Camel, two of them exit while the third moves regally across the front of the sanctuary, accompanying the following reading.

READER   "The Camels Speak" by Lynn Ungar:

Of course they never consulted us.
They were wise men, kings, star-readers,
and we merely transportation.
They simply loaded us with gifts
and turned us toward the star.
I ask you, what would a king know
of choosing presents for a child?
Had they ever even seen a baby
born to such simple folks,
so naked of pretension,
so open to the wind?
What would such a child care
for perfumes and gold? Far better
to have asked one born in the desert,
tested by wind and sand. We saw
what he would need: the gift
of perseverance, of continuing on the hard way,
making do with what there is,
living on what you have inside.

The gift of holding up under a burden,
of lifting another with grace, of kneeling

To accept the weight of what you must bear.
Our footsteps could have rocked him
with the rhythm of the road,
shown him comfort in a harsh land,
the dignity of continually moving forward.
But the wise men were not
wise enough to ask. They simply
left their trinkets and admired
the rustic view. Before you knew it
we were turned again toward home,
carrying men only half-willing
to be amazed. But never mind.
We saw the baby, felt him reach
for the bright tassels of our gear.
We desert amblers have our ways
of seeing what you chatterers must miss.
That child at heart knows something
about following a star. Our gifts are given.
Have no doubt. His life will bear
the print of who we are.

The Reader and the Camel exit as Azadeh, Lilya, and Tehmina (and their Camels, if they have them) arrive and settle themselves around the family. Lilya stirs a cooking pot with a spoon, offering sips to Mary and Joseph. Tehmina plumps beautiful pillows, drapes a blanket over baby Jesus, and perhaps tucks a shawl around Mary.

AZADEH [*addresses congregation*] We were amazed. We arrived at that humble stable, and we were amazed to the point of being changed. Tehmina, Lilya, and I all knew something about "making do with what there is" and accepting the weight of what we must bear. And in the eyes of that baby, we saw that he knew, too. There was no question that he understood suffering, even at a few days old. I sensed somehow that his life would both relieve the suffering of others . . . and end in his own suffering. We were changed by this child, and received something from him, even though we came to give of ourselves. And we did what we came to do: each of us presented our gift to Mary, to Joseph, and to their plump, precious son resting in the manger. We fortified the new parents with rich broth, and prepared them a comfortable bed in the stable. All of the visitors had left. The cows and sheep were our only companions within the stable walls. As the stars shined their light through the night, Mary and Joseph spoke the quiet language of love to their newborn, cradling him and cooing to him as the family settled into sleep—and I sang them my lullaby.

Without speaking, the Leader indicates that the entire congregation is to sing this hymn. The actors remain, pretending to sleep or to watch vigil over the family, during and after the hymn.

"**Sleep, My Child**," *SLT,* 409

LEADER   Tonight, the moon will keep her watch over us, while half the world sleeps. May we who are awake keep our loving vigil over one another. May this pure and holy feeling linger in us, through this night and the many that follow.

Note: If you use this as a Christmas Eve service, you can add a final element—lighting candles and singing "Silent Night," SLT, 251.

The Blue-Green Hills of Earth
Earth Day

An important part of Unitarian Universalism is the sense of mystery and wonder that triggers a "wow!" feeling inside us. This Earth Day (April 22) service uses the congregation's imagination and a system of maps to draw our gaze outward, from our street, to our city, to our state—all the way to our Milky Way galaxy. This service contains special suggestions for those congregations interested in projecting images using Power Point or Keynote software programs.

Preparation (significant)

- This service will be most effective with some complementary activities in the religious education program, the social justice committee, and similar church programs. For example, your congregation could hold a "bike to church" day or a composting Sunday, show the documentary film *An Inconvenient Truth*, make reusable shopping bags (see www.earthdaybags.com), or install bat boxes on the property.

- Announce ahead of time that this service will include a Recycling Offering: each person/family should bring a recyclable item, such as a plastic water bottle or an empty soda can. (Note that after the service, the service coordinator will be responsible for making sure the items actually get recycled!)

- If you want to "walk the talk" of environmental stewardship, decide whether to forgo printing the order of service for this Sunday.

- Prepare a list of small ways to be environmentally conscious: turn off lights when you leave the room, bring your own mug to coffee hour, give rides to friends, etc. Print the list on a large dry-erase board or chalkboard. If using projection technology with this service, you may include this list as a slide in the Power Point or Keynote presentation, outlined below.

- If not using projection technology, find an Earth flag or a poster with a photograph of the Earth taken from space.

- If not using projection technology, find a poster of the famous 1990 photograph called the "pale blue dot," taken by NASA's Voyager 1 spacecraft.

- If using projection technology, obtain a screen to project images onto. Create a Power Point or Keynote presentation. It should display the following slides in this order:

  - Lyrics to "Blue Boat Home," *STJ*, 1064.
  - Photograph of the Earth taken from space.
  - Lyrics to "For the Earth Forever Turning," *SLT*, 163.
  - Several images that illustrate the text read by Reader D and Reader E. Consult that text for inspiration. The series of images should begin with the solar system and end with the "pale blue dot" photograph, which is easy to find online. Suggestions for others images include Carl Sagan, the NASA logo, Voyager 1, and the Milky Way galaxy.
  - List of small ways to be environmentally conscious (see above).
  - Lyrics for "This Is My Song," *SLT*, 159.

- If you'd like to incorporate more media into the service and are using projection technology, make a DVD of one of the music videos available from Symphony of Science (www.symphonyofscience.com) to show during the Offering.

- Obtain a poster-size map of each of the following: your town or city, your city's region or county, your state, your section of the United States, the United States, and the world. Also obtain a poster of the solar system and of the Milky Way galaxy. Clip them all to an easel. The Milky Way poster should be clipped on first, at the back of the stack, and the rest should be stacked in descending order by size, with your town or city's map showing on the front of the stack. Put star or dot stickers near the easel.

- Buy chocolates wrapped in foil to look like the Earth. These are available at many food co-ops and natural food stores.

- Place a clearly marked receptacle for recycling at the front of the sanctuary.

- *Rehearsal will take about 1 hour.*

Roles (5, all should attend rehearsal)

5 Readers

As the service begins, the easel with maps, the stickers, the dry-erase board, and the container for recycling are in place, and a photo of the Earth is hanging in or projected onto a clearly visible spot. Reader A is at the front.

Welcome

Reader A welcomes congregants and visitors.

READER A Our Unitarian Universalist Principles affirm that, from fruit flies to giant sequoia trees, all life is interwoven and interconnected. That interdependence moves us to a sense of awe, and invites us to care for the life that moves among us. Today, as a community of all generations, we celebrate our place in this earthly home, with its skies and seas, and its blue-green hills. Let us begin this hour by lighting the symbol of Unitarian Universalism.

Chalice Lighting

READER B   Happy Earth Day! This morning we celebrate this planet of ours, spinning through space, circling the sun. Before we talk about where on Earth we are, and how to care for our planet, let us practice gratitude. Earth is home to our human family and to millions of other creatures: animals, insects, plants, flowers, birds . . . and our opening words will be an expression of thanks for all of them. Do you think we could name every animal and insect and plant and flower if we spent this entire hour on it? [*allows some responses from the congregation*]

It would take too long; there are just too many living things on our planet. But do you think that we could name just twenty-six creatures that share our Earth—one for every letter of the alphabet? [*gets the congregation's agreement*]

Let's try it. We should make sure that we don't lose our place in the alphabet, though. Is there anyone who'd like to join me up here to be our alphabet leader, so that we go through the alphabet in the right order? [*Reader B chooses a young volunteer. If the child is eager but nervous, parents can be invited forward too. Reader B sets the gentle expectation that—out of fairness—people will raise their hands to be called on.*]

On this [Earth Day/Earth Day weekend], we remember and give thanks for these creatures: [*Reader B asks the volunteer what letter comes first, then calls on someone who can offer an animal or flower—or any part of nature—that begins with the letter A, then B, then C, and so on. Eventually, the volunteer may help call on people. After each item is named—"apples" or "bumblebees"—Reader B provides an affirmation by saying, "Thank you, Earth, for apples" or "We give thanks for bumblebees." When the alphabet is done, Reader B thanks the volunteer.*]

Phew! We did it! Those are all important things to be grateful for, and a reminder that we aren't the only ones on this planet. In that spirit, let us sing our opening hymn . . .

If using projection technology, display lyrics to the following hymn.

"**Blue Boat Home**," *STJ,* 1064

READER C   If we're going to try to think about our "blue boat home" with wonder and awe, we should start there: What do awe and wonder feel like? [*allows a few descriptions*]

Wonder is the feeling that gives us goosebumps, and makes us say, "Wow." It's the feeling we get when we start thinking about questions with no answers. Here's how the first Source of our Unitarian Universalist tradition describes it: "direct experience of that transcending mystery and wonder, affirmed in all cultures, which moves us to a renewal of the spirit and an openness to the forces which create and uphold life."

We're going to see whether we can invite those feelings by using maps. The maps on this easel—and you—are going to help us remember our place on this blue-green planet, and find our place in the universe. Let's start with this map on top. What does this map show? [*waits for someone to identify the top map as your town or city, pointing out major identifying characteristics if needed*]

Would someone like to come forward and mark our [church/fellowship] on this map? [*helps a child or youth place a sticker on the congregation's location on the map and invites the congregation to thank the volunteer*]

This map shows us what we'd see if we were above our town, like a giant bird looking down, or if we were a satellite camera in the sky. We can see all of the roads, parks, and bodies of water that we'd see from above. What would our corner of Earth look like if we went up higher, to get a bigger view? [*flips town map back to reveal a map of the region, such as the county or a portion of the state*]

Will another volunteer come forward and show us where our congregation is on this map? [*invites a volunteer up and helps her to find the congregation's vicinity and put a sticker on it*]

We're going to keep moving outward to see an even broader view of where we live. [*flips to the map of the state or province, selects a volunteer, marks the congregation's general area, and invites thanks*]

We're doing pretty well! Let's move out farther, and look at our country. [*with a map of the country revealed, solicits the help of yet another volunteer*]

So far, these maps have shown the land of our own country ... but there's a much bigger world out there than just us. Here's a map of the world—can anyone find our congregation on this map? [*calls on a volunteer of a different age than the previous volunteers and thanks him when he is finished*]

Maps were created by humans to show certain information about land, rivers, and roads. They also show borders between states and between countries—but those borders are also human inventions. So far, all the maps we've seen today have shown our city, our country, or our world with those artificial boundaries. But there's a different way of looking at our world, with no dotted lines or declarations about who owns what land. [*indicates the view of Earth from space, whether poster, Earth flag, or slide*]

What about this view is different from all the other things we've seen so far? What do you see here that we can't see on the maps? [*asks for ideas from the congregation, allowing both technical and artistic responses*]

How do you feel when you look at this photograph? [*allows a significant number of people to name how they feel when they see our Earth from space*]

Here's a pretty interesting fact: For most of our history, we human beings didn't have this view of Earth. Even though we've been looking up at the stars for hundreds of thousands of years, we had to imagine what Earth looked like. Nobody knew exactly what our planet looked like until 1966, when the U.S. Lunar Orbiter 1 caught its first small peek of our planet. Six years later, in 1972, the crew of Apollo 17 took the most well-known picture of Earth, a photograph called "The Blue Marble" by the astronauts. Even though 1972 sounds like a long time ago, it's not. Just to show how new this view of Earth is, please raise your hand if you were born before this picture was taken (and are willing to admit it). [*waits for responses*]

That's how new this view of our planet is. And that 1972 trip was the last time any humans have visited the moon. Do you think the moon is lonely for our company? Let's keep this image of Earth in mind as we sing our next hymn, "For the Earth Forever Turning."

If using projection technology, display lyrics to the following hymn.

"For the Earth Forever Turning," SLT, 163

READER D   That hymn, by composer Kim Oler, is an ode to "our blue-green hills of Earth." Our home planet does have blue-green hills, but when we see Earth from space—a view similar to what you see here—we can also see tan deserts, indigo oceans, and ivory cloud cover. Let's keep traveling outward, beyond Earth, and see where we fit into the cosmos. [*Reader D flips the world map back to show the poster of the solar system, or a projector is used to begin a slide show, beginning with the solar system. If the poster is used, Reader D asks for a volunteer to come forward yet again to stick a star or dot on our planet. If the slide show is used, a volunteer can point to Earth. The slide show can continue, as Reader D speaks, to show the Milky Way, the NASA logo, Carl Sagan, and other images.*]

There's no way to find our country, much less our city, in this poster of the solar system! But we're still part of it. We're in that picture, whether we can see ourselves or not. Why do you think it's important to know that we're there, in that photo? [*allows some time for answers, then flips to the next poster, showing the Milky Way galaxy*]

Here's the Milky Way galaxy, where our solar system is located. There are hundreds of billions of solar systems like ours in this galaxy. Some people feel very small when they see the Milky Way galaxy and realize our tiny place in it. Some people feel tingly inside, or goose-bumpy on the outside. That's why it was important for us to try to see Earth from outer space . . . and our next story is about an astronomer who knew that. Does anyone know what NASA is? What does NASA do? [*waits for someone to name the National Aeronautics and Space Administration or explain that NASA is responsible for our country's space program*]

NASA designs the spacecraft and shuttles that travel into space and to the international space station. In the 1970s, NASA asked a scientist named Carl Sagan to help them design spacecraft. One of them was called Voyager 1. Voyager was designed to go very, very far into outer space—way past the moon—a trip so long that it would take many, many years (that's one reason there were no people on board). In fact, Voyager is still on its trip; it's farther from Earth than any other human-made object. Before it left our solar system, Voyager gave us a present—thanks to Carl Sagan. Carl loved astronomy, but he had ideas that went beyond how to build space ships. He decided that it was very important for us, on Earth, to see our planet from far away. Carl told NASA that they should program Voyager's camera to take a picture of our planet from the edge of our solar system. The photo of Earth that we just looked at was taken from [the moon/space]. It's beautiful, and it shows details of the blue-green hills and oceans. But the people at NASA told Carl that a picture taken from the edge of the solar system—3.7 billion miles away—would be useless, because Earth would be so tiny. Carl didn't give up. In the months leading up to Voyager's launch, he begged and pleaded NASA for the photograph to be taken. He wouldn't let them say no, and he finally got his way. In the spring of 1990, as the Voyager spacecraft was speeding out of our solar system at 40,000 miles per hour, it turned its cameras back towards Earth for "one last glance homeward." [*indicates "pale blue dot" poster, or slide show reveals the "pale blue dot" picture, which remains on while Reader E speaks*] The Voyager picture shows Earth as a tiny pinprick of light sitting alone in a vast darkness. Through an accident of geometry and optics, Earth seems to be sitting in a beam of light. The planet itself emits a light blue glow, thanks to our seas and skies. This awe-inspiring picture is affectionately called the "pale blue dot." Carl Sagan knew that seeing Earth as a tiny blue dot in space would be important for humans. He was right. This is how Carl explained his sense of awe:

READER E   Look at that dot. . . . That's here, that's home, that's us. On that dot everyone you love, everyone you know, everyone you ever heard of, every human being who ever lived, lived out their lives. . . . Every hunter and forager, every hero and coward, every creator and destroyer of civilization, every king and peasant, every young couple in love, every mother and father, every hopeful child, every inventor and explorer, every revered teacher of morals, every corrupt politician, every superstar, every supreme leader, every saint and sinner in the history of our species lived there on a mote of dust suspended in a sunbeam. The earth is a very small stage in a vast cosmic arena. . . . Our planet is a lonely speck in a great enveloping cosmic dark. In our obscurity, in all this vastness there is no hint that help will come from elsewhere to save us from ourselves, it is up to us. . . . For me it underscores our responsibility, our profound responsibility, to deal more kindly with one another and to preserve and cherish that pale blue dot, the only home we have ever known.

End slide show, until list of recycling tips is needed.

READER B Those are big thoughts. It can seem like a big job, and a big responsibility, to take care of our pale blue planet and all that lives here. Today, we asked you to bring a piece of recycling for a Recycling Offering. Who's got a recycling bin at home? [*waits for people to raise hands*]

You could have put your one piece of recycling into your bin at home, but putting it all together is a way to remind ourselves of what happens when we all join together. If every piece of recycling you have with you is a promise to do one small thing to help the environment, then imagine what we can do right here.

What are some ways that we can be good caretakers of the Earth? [*asks for suggestions from the congregation*] I have a list here with some of those ideas, and more. [*refers to chalkboard or projection screen; reads a few that haven't been named yet*]

It's time for our recycling offering. If you brought a piece of recycling, please bring it forward and put it in the container. As you put it in, please try to tell us one thing that you can do to help the Earth.

Reader B allows time for people to come forward, one at a time or all at once. Large congregations in which a "communion" for individuals may be unwieldy might instead pass large baskets through the aisles and invite people to tell their neighbors what they can promise to do as Earth caretakers.

When the offering has been brought forward:

READER C   Wow! That's a lot of recycling . . . and it's a lot of community power! May we help each other remember our promises to the Earth. Just as importantly, may we look to the skies once in a while, to remember why we've made those promises. We make a difference by coming together, one by one, and putting our strength together. That's true in taking care of the Earth, and it's also true in caring for our congregation and its programs in our larger community. Now that you've practiced giving away your sticky bottles and your crumpled papers, you get to practice giving away something that's harder to part with: a portion of your resources. Let us give in gladness this morning, knowing that our community is nurtured by our generosity—and in exchange for your giving, you'll receive a special treat! [*asks for 2 volunteers to follow behind the offering baskets and hand out chocolates*]

Offering

If you wish, show one of the Symphony of Science music videos during Offering.

READER A   As we find a moment of quiet together, think of something that creates awe inside you. What gives you a sense of wonder? What are you most grateful for? Take a moment to think about the sources of your awe and amazement.

[*after a moment*] As we prepare to end our service, please help me create a prayer of thanks for the gifts of life that fill us with wonder. When I ring the chime, please speak out loud the things you just thought about, so that our voices blend to create a patchwork of thanks for these gifts.

[*waits until voices have grown quiet*] Thank you, Spirit of Life, for the mystery and miracle of our connection to life—and to one another.

Please join me in singing, with care and promise, "This Is My Song."

If using projection technology, display lyrics to the following hymn.

"This Is My Song," *SLT,* 159

READER A   These are the words of Walt Whitman, from *Leaves of Grass*:

When I heard the learn'd astronomer;
When the proofs, the figures, were ranged in columns before me;
When I was shown the charts and the diagrams, to add, divide, and measure them;
When I, sitting, heard the astronomer, where he lectured with much applause in the lecture-room,

How soon, unaccountable, I became tired and sick;
Till rising and gliding out, I wander'd off by myself,
In the mystical moist night-air, and from time to time,
Look'd up in perfect silence at the stars.

Go out in peace, remembering to look up and remember the stars.

Note: At the end of this service, you might "reuse" the maps by giving them away, reminding people that they make great wrapping paper and homemade envelopes.

Good News, Bad News
Bridging Ceremony

Imagine that you have a beloved horse, and that she has just run away. Quick—is that good news or bad news? Are you sure? This Chinese folk tale reminds us not to label things too quickly, because whether an event is wonderful or tragic sometimes changes according to the context. This story reminds us that life is full of changes and surprises. How can we meet life's twists and turns with hope? What does our Unitarian Universalist tradition teach us about our power to create happy endings? This service includes a bridging ceremony to honor graduating high school seniors, but it can also be modified for use on a regular Sunday.

Preparation (moderate)

- Prepare small gifts for the bridging youth, perhaps a membership to the Church of the Younger Fellowship (www.uucyf.org).

- Print words and music to "Take My Hand" in order of service (see page 46).

- Working with your director of religious education, find an adult to present those who are bridging with a brief paragraph describing each of them, their gifts, and their next step after high school (whether it's college, a job, traveling, etc.). While you might also ask the youth to speak for themselves, many high school students will feel pressured by this and prefer to have a trusted adult speak on their behalf.

- Make 2 large signs, one with a happy face and one with a sad face.
- Obtain 2 stuffed horses, hobby horses, horse masks, or other costumes. One is the farmer's horse; the other is the wild horse.
- Outfit the soldiers with swords and armor.
- Fill a few baskets with pens.
- Make paper cutouts shaped like footprints and put one in each order of service.
- Recruit volunteer(s) to distribute pens.
- Check with your congregation's leadership to make sure it's okay to post in a public place all the "footprints" that people will fill out.
- Reserve seats in the front row for the actors.
- *Rehearsal will take about 1 hour.*

Roles (7–8, those who need to attend rehearsal are marked with *)

- Leader*
- Storyteller* (the Leader may also serve as the Storyteller)
- Farmer*
- Horse* (manipulates one or two horses, as indicated)
- Farmer's Son*
- 2–3 Soldiers

Welcome

The Leader welcomes congregants and visitors.

LEADER Have you ever heard someone say, "I have bad news and good news—which one do you want to hear first?" What do you choose to hear first, when someone offers you those two options? [*allows congregation to respond*]

Here's some good news—this morning we're going to hear a story that invites us to change the way we think about good news and bad news, a story that reminds us to honor the paths that our lives take, however twisty and turn-y those paths are. This story comes from the tradition of Chinese wisdom stories: tales that have been told for many generations in Chinese culture, because inside their playful details there's a nugget of truth that can be meaningful to all of us. This morning we're also going to honor our graduating high school seniors and this important step in their life journeys. So you might say that there's no real bad news to report at this time. Please join me in singing our opening song, whose lyrics call us back to the starting point of our journeys.

"Return Again," *STJ,* 1011

LEADER   Once again, as with so many other mornings,
our lives have brought us to this place:
this holy ground of being and becoming;
crucible of revelation and relationship;
harbor of religious community.
Let us open ourselves to the morning, set our lives aside for these moments,
and gather the strength to move forward into the life that calls us.

Chalice Lighting

STORYTELLER   Before we begin our story, "Good News, Bad News," I need to ask your help, because you're going to be the villagers in our story. It's an easy and fun part! Here's how you'll know what to say, and when: I have two signs. When I hold up the "happy" sign, please exclaim happily about what good news you've heard. If I hold up the "sad" sign, please moan and lament the bad news you've heard. Shall we practice? Tonight for dinner you'll have nothing to eat but ice cream! [*holds up "happy" sign and allows congregation to respond for a moment*]

Oops. I'm sorry, but it turns out that your freezer is unplugged right now, and your ice cream is melting, so there will be nothing for dinner after all! [*holds up "sad" sign, inviting them to now moan and complain*]

Great—you've learned your part! Before we begin our story, let's sing together to get our speaking voices ready.

"When the Spirit Says Do," *STJ*, 1024

Note: You might add verses that say "you've got to cheer . . ." and "you've got to cry . . ."

STORYTELLER You know how to play your role, and we've warmed up our voices. Let's begin our story, "Good News, Bad News."

Farmer and Horse enter and act out the following passage. While reading, the Storyteller allows time for the acting to unfold.

Once there was a farmer who owned a beautiful horse. She loved this horse and spent long hours caring for it. In fact, the farmer's horse was widely admired; the people of her village would often stop as they walked by to gaze upon it and comment on its beauty. One afternoon the farmer rode her beloved horse in from the fields after a day of work. But in her haste, she didn't fully close the gate to the corral. That evening, as the moon rose up over the pasture and the farmer slept in her house, the beautiful and precious horse pushed open the gate, running away quickly toward the forest and into the far-reaching trees. The next morning as the sun rose, the farmer discovered the empty corral. Villagers walking past the corral also noticed that it was empty. Word that the beloved horse had escaped spread quickly among the farmer's neighbors. [*holds up the "sad" sign and allows the congregation to respond*]

But the farmer just said:

FARMER Maybe it's good, maybe it's bad. It's too soon to tell.

STORYTELLER The villagers were certain that the horse would never return, and that the farmer was stubbornly not accepting her loss. Days passed, until one afternoon at dusk the farmer's horse emerged from the forest, trotting back towards the corral . . . and the neighbors were stunned to see that a herd of wild horses was following the farmer's horse!

Horse returns, manipulating two horse puppets: the farmer's horse and the wild horse. The rest of the "herd" is imagined.

All of the horses found their way into the corral, and to the trough of food waiting there. This time, the farmer was sure to lock her gate. Word of this turn of events quickly spread among the villagers, and the farmer's neighbors came to celebrate. [*holds up "happy" sign*]

But the farmer said only:

FARMER   Maybe it's good, maybe it's bad. It's too soon to tell.

Farmer and Horse sit down in the front row seats.

LEADER   We'll continue this interesting story in a moment. So far, our villagers have celebrated a happy situation, and have offered sympathy for a sad one. In this way, they're similar to our community: In this congregation, we care deeply enough about each other that another person's sorrow becomes ours to mourn. Someone else's joy is ours to celebrate. Our listening to joys and sorrows is a way of healing, and weaving our hearts together. Let us share this time together with open hearts.

Joys and Sorrows

After the congregation has shared, the Leader calls for a period of silent meditation and allows at least a minute of silence.

Whether the coming days bring us joy or sorrow, may the deep peace and love of this community sustain us.

"Come Sing a Song With Me," *SLT*, 346

Farmer and Farmer's Son take their places in front. From this point forward the Farmer's Son animates the wild horse.

STORYTELLER   When we paused in our story, the farmer's horse had just returned to the corral, bringing a herd of wild horses. The farmer enjoyed watching this new herd of horses in her corral. Her grown son enjoyed them even more. He had been watching them with admiration. One of the wild horses in particular—a beautiful horse that looked as if she could run as fast as the wind—fascinated him. He decided to try to break the wild horse, and train her to ride with him on her back. But that afternoon, as he tried to break her, the horse threw the son. He landed heavily on the ground, breaking both of his legs. [*holds up "sad" sign*]

As you can guess, the farmer had just one thing to say:

FARMER   Maybe it's good, maybe it's bad. It's too soon to tell.

STORYTELLER   The villagers were still clucking and tsk-tsk-tsk-ing about the son's broken legs and how terrible this accident was when from the distance . . . can you hear it? . . . the thundering of more horse hooves could be heard entering the village. This time, it wasn't a herd of wild horses, but the Emperor's troops riding down the valley, flags flapping in the air, armor gleaming in the sun.

Two or three Soldiers enter, ad-libbing phrases such as, "Calling all men to war!" etc. and acting out the following scene.

As the troops wound their way from farm to farm, they announced the news of a war in the far edges of the country. It was a large war effort, so every able-bodied young man in the country was being conscripted. When they reached the farmer's house, they found her injured son and left him behind, excusing him from being conscripted, because his legs were still healing. Even as they mourned the departure of their healthy sons, the neighbors came to celebrate with the farmer that her son was safe from being made a soldier. [*holds up "happy" sign*]

And how do you think the farmer responded? [*gestures for congregation to join in and say the following line, along with Farmer and the Storyteller*]

FARMER/STORYTELLER   Maybe it's good, maybe it's bad. It's too soon to tell.

STORYTELLER As you can imagine, this story of ours could go on and on, but we'll end it here, on a happy note. Let's thank the actors who helped bring the story to life.

Actors take their seats.

LEADER How wonderful! How terrible! How confusing! The candles we lit this morning illustrate the fact that our lives are always absorbing new joys and sorrows. Our paths are continually shaped by good news and bad news, as we try to make sense of the new direction we're given. The folk tale that we just heard echoes something else that we already know: life takes strange turns. Life throws us curve balls. Life contains surprises that we never saw coming, and aren't sure what to do with. Maybe you've learned that, sometimes, good news turns out to be not-so-good after all; sometimes the things we hope for, and reach for, don't bring us the happiness we expect. We know that sometimes bad news is just that, plain and simple: an utter tragedy from which it's hard to heal. But once in a while, bad news can open the door for growth. Sometimes, sorrows can lead us places we never could have imagined.

How wonderful! How terrible! How confusing! Ever since human beings could formulate questions about life and the Great Mysterious, we've wondered: Why do our paths take such sudden turns? And when those turns happen, we struggle to know: How do we respond to life's curve balls? As Unitarian Universalists, we don't have a fixed answer to questions about why our paths twist and turn so suddenly. Do you believe that the Spirit of Life has planned your life journey? Do you believe that fate, or karma, has mapped out the direction of your life? Are we guided along our journey at all, or is the road in front of us open in every direction, shaped only by our free will?

These questions form the mystery in which we move and breathe and dwell; for every person here, there may be a different answer. But we ask the questions freely, and embrace them as part of the journey. When we stumble upon hard-won answers, we remember that what each person knows is a piece of the truth. How, then, do we ride those mysterious waves of joy and sorrow?

In our story, most of us were pretty sure whether the story was turning happy or sad. But the farmer had the same response to each surprise: "Maybe it's good, maybe it's bad. It's too soon to tell." It's as if she were saying, I don't know how this story ends, so I'm going to bear witness to this piece of it without jumping ahead and drawing conclusions.

In the paths that our lives take, there's both pain and glory in the not-knowing. When seen up close, our small steps may lead to nowhere but confusion. It's not until we step back that we see, through the gift of time or perspective, the topography of our journeys. Our Unitarian Universalist tradition invites us to observe that larger journey with compassion, and to make meaning from it. We challenge ourselves to believe in the goodness of life, the importance of justice, and the power of hope. And we believe that every sudden swerve into mystery is made gentler by having a beloved community. We don't have to do it alone. As the paths of our lives continue to unfold, may we be good companions to one another, and may our journeys bring us meaning and hope.

Please join me in singing our hymn, "Take My Hand," which you'll find as an insert in your order of service. This simple chant was written by a Unitarian Universalist named Jennifer Hazel, for the 2001 bridging ceremony held at our General Assembly.

"Take My Hand," verses 1–3 [*music on page 46*]

If skipping the bridging ceremony, sing all five verses now, then pick up the script just below "Take My Hand" verses 4–5.

LEADER   This morning, we pause to recognize the youth in our community who are taking an important step in their own journeys, and moving forward into their futures. [*Names of seniors*] are all graduating from high school this month. Many of you have watched these youth grow up, and sheltered them with your love. In a moment, we'll hear about each one of our seniors—but first, a reminder: these youth are now stepping into young adulthood.

[*addresses youth*] [*Names*], you are going out into the world, but we're not sending you away. This is your congregation—and you're welcome to return here always and forever. In the coming years, your life journeys will inevitably twist towards sorrow, and detour back into joy. Whether it's to seek comfort or celebration, we hope that you'll be led back to us, your spiritual home, from time to time.

Each youth is briefly introduced to the congregation by an adult, given their gift, and celebrated.

LEADER   *"Bridging Prayer" by Donna DiSciullo, adapted:*

Oh Love That Will Not Let Us Go,
we gather in this community to honor our young people,
who have touched our lives and our congregation with their
    creativity,
with their boundless energy, with their love.
We gather, filled with hope and confidence,
for they are our future, as well as our present.
As they venture out into a larger world,
may they carry with them faith in the power of love to change the
    world,
the realization that what they do matters greatly,
an understanding of how acts of love and justice connect us to
    each other.
May they love the world and bless it with their lives.
For those on the far side of the Bridge—
who have known the uncertainty of change,
who have experienced the grace of community,
who have felt the love and reaped the gifts—
may you remember . . . and reach out.
May all present honor our young adults with acts of commitment
    and courage, compassion and continuity.
Oh Love That Will Not Let Us Go, bless each of our journeys,
and make us good companions to one another.

"Take My Hand," verses 4–5 [*music on page 46*]

LEADER Think back for a moment on the paths that your life has taken. The gift of time often allows us to see where our journeys have unfolded, clearly and straight-forwardly, and where our paths have taken mysterious twists and turns. In this part of our service, I invite you to consider the surprises and the curve balls of your life—whether it was good news that turned sour, or bad news that opened a door. Along the path of your life, which surprise can you look back to, full of gratitude? Take a minute or two now to reflect. If you're a parent, please talk to your child or youth about surprises that he or she is grateful for. *[pauses to allow the congregation to reflect]*

Inside your order of service, you will find a paper footprint. We're going to pass out pens now, for those who need them, and I'm going to ask you to write down that unexpected step that you're grateful for. These footprints will be put up along our sanctuary wall later today, in a series of curving paths. Your footprint will bear witness to the paths that lie behind us . . . and will serve as a message of hope to others, as each of us continues to receive new surprises into our lives.

Volunteers pass out baskets of pens while music plays softly. The Leader allows time for people to finish writing. If there's time remaining in the service, the Leader can ask people to volunteer to stand and read what they've written.

Thank you for sharing this piece of your life with your community. You already share so much of yourself with our congregation: your life wisdom, your time, and your talents. As we collect this morning's offering, please put your footprint in the basket as an affirmation of your place among us, and please put in your offering as an affirmation of generosity and outreach.

Offering

LEADER Just as the farmer discovered, and just as your footprints bear witness, more surprise turns await us on life's path. Our closing hymn reminds us to have faith that we'll get there, and that we'll do it together.

"Woyaya," *STJ,* 1020

LEADER In the coming days . . . and weeks . . . and years,
There will be times when the path before you is clear;
There will be times when the path is so foggy that your next step will feel scary.
When the way is clear, may you offer hope and strength to others.
And when the path is uncertain, may there be an outstretched hand to hold yours.

After the service, hang the congregation's footprints on the sanctuary wall, in a series of forking paths.

Take My Hand

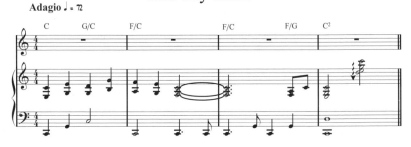
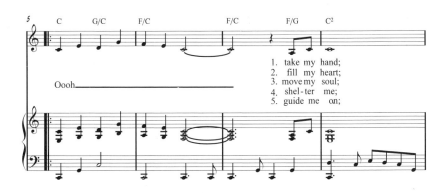
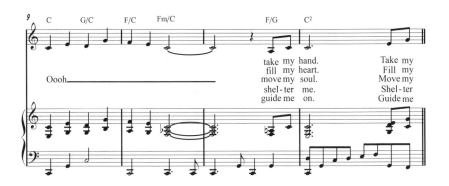

Melody and verses 1-3 © Jennifer Hazel (all rights reserved);
additional lyrics by Erika Hewitt;
harmonization and arrangement by John Douglas & Erika Hewitt;
this arrangement © 2008

The Creator's Workshop

In this very interactive service based on the story "A Little Jar Labeled Freedom" by Rev. Cynthia B. Johnson, we witness one story of our planet's birth, in which humans are given the precious gift of freedom. When is our freedom to choose one thing instead of the other frightening? When does it feel especially juicy, and ripe with promise? How do we use our freedom wisely?

Preparation (significant)

- Create a set for the Creator's workshop at the front of the sanctuary: Set up a card table, with a very large mixing bowl or punch bowl on top. At the back place another table, stand, or bookcase containing lots of small boxes, tins, jars, and envelopes. You might wrap tiny Christmas lights in colored netting around the mixing bowl, or hang complicated mathematical posters on the wall, or, for humor, have the Creator don safety goggles and a helmet before beginning—or anything else to jazz up the workshop in a whimsical way.

- Fill the small containers, separately, with water, blue ribbons, leaves, twigs, dirt, feathers, and unscented baby powder, confetti, or sparkly fairy dust, and label them so that the Creator will know what is in them. Use something like salt shakers for emotions and senses. Label one jar "Freedom."

- Obtain a packet of seeds, a small variety of stuffed animals, 2 picture frames (at least 8 x 10"), a parachute or very long bolt of cloth, an inflatable globe or Earth ball, and a rainstick.

- Fill several small baskets with Hershey's kisses or chocolates wrapped in foil to look like Earth.

- Plant some volunteers in the congregation to begin singing the first hymn from their seats.

- *Rehearsal will take between 2 and 3 hours.*

Roles (4, all should attend rehearsal)

- Storyteller

- Questioner

- Universe

- Creator

As the service begins, Creator's workshop is in place at the front of the sanctuary, and the Storyteller is standing at the pulpit.

STORYTELLER   For as long as we've been on our planet Earth, human beings have asked important questions. Some of them are easy to answer, like why birds fly south in the winter (because it's too far to walk, of course). Other questions aren't at all easy to answer. The world's religions have tried to answer those questions, each in its own way, usually by telling stories to explain where we come from, who we are, and where we're going. We're about to tell you one of those stories.

Questioner and Universe enter together, talking.

QUESTIONER   [*to Universe, in a conversational tone*] Where do we come from? What are we? Where are we going?

UNIVERSE   [*replying earnestly*] Mystery . . . Mystery . . . Life is a riddle and a mystery.

QUESTIONER   Where do we come from? What are we? Where are we going?

UNIVERSE   Mystery . . . Mystery . . . Life is a riddle and a mystery.

QUESTIONER   [*beginning to match rhythm to line 2 of "Where Do We Come From," hymn 1003 in Singing the Journey*] Where do we come from? Where do we come from?

UNIVERSE   [*matching the rhythm to line 3 of the hymn*] Mystery . . . Mystery . . . Life is a riddle and a mystery.

Both Questioner and Universe repeat their lines at the same time, "speak-singing" the hymn's lines, about five or six times. The accompanist begins to softly play the notes that are being spoken (one or both of the lines). As the accompanist continues to play the notes softly, individuals in the congregation begin to sing each of the four lines from the hymn, gradually bringing the congregation into full song.

"Where Do We Come From," *STJ,* 1003

Welcome

Questioner welcomes congregants and visitors.

QUESTIONER   We're about to travel to the workshop of a Creator and hear a story about how we came to be; how we human beings got the ability to make choices and accept the consequences of those choices. You should know that, in this service, you'll be asked not just to watch and listen, but also to contribute your feelings and thoughts to our story. Please be ready to jump in, to share, and to immerse yourself fully in worship. Let us open the door to our story by lighting our chalice.

Chalice Lighting

With the kindling of this flame,
we honor the mysteries and riddles that prompt us to ask
    questions;
we give thanks for this community, in which we can seek their
    answers,
and we open our hearts and minds to our great and many
    freedoms.

Universe lights chalice.

Creator enters and stands at her table. Universe and Questioner stand on either side of the front of the sanctuary, watching Creator work during the following narration. The Storyteller remains at the pulpit/microphone throughout the scene.

STORYTELLER Once upon a time, long, long ago, there was a Creator who had a hobby of making planets. The Creator took pride in making each one different. One day she looked at a gap in the solar system and pondered it.

CREATOR I think I'll make a planet to go over there. Let me think . . . how will I make this one?

STORYTELLER She sat and looked out into the vast reaches of swirling matter and thought long and hard about creating another new planet. She had a very large workshop, in which she had rows and rows of shelves, with little jars and envelopes of things.

Creator rifles through jars, cans, and boxes.

To begin, she took a large glass jar down from the shelf and started adding ingredients to her planet—a pinch of this, a pinch of that.

Creator begins "cooking" up a planet.

She poured in lots of liquid from the jar marked "Oceans and Seas."

Creator and Universe pull blue ribbons out of a jar, or otherwise add to the oceans. Questioner tips rainstick back and forth. The Storyteller pauses to allow for complete sound.

From the jar marked "Clear Lakes," she slowly poured in more liquid, topping it off with a drop from a jar labeled "Waterfalls."

QUESTIONER [*to congregation*] What are some of your favorite rivers and lakes and seas?

Questioner waits for members of the congregation to call out the bodies of water that are special to them, as Creator continues to add them to the mixing bowl, perhaps acknowledging the names and taking them as suggestions.

STORYTELLER   The Creator smiled and then added mountains, forests and jungles to her new planet.

Creator flings in leaves, twigs, etc. into the mixing bowl, then sprinkles in dirt from a jar, empties in a seed packet, etc.

QUESTIONER   [*to congregation*] Which mountains and forests are you grateful to have on our planet?

The congregation names their favorite places while Creator adds them.

STORYTELLER   Then she added a dash of furry and feathered animals.

As Creator drops feathers, etc., into her mixing bowl, Universe and Questioner begin to pass out a few stuffed animals to the congregation with comments like, "Aren't we lucky to have dogs?" and "Oh, a penguin—my favorite." The Storyteller pauses long enough so that the congregation is encouraged to cuddle the animals and pass them on.

STORYTELLER   Then she decided to shake in a sample from among her boxes, labeled "Human Beings."

All actors freeze as Questioner approaches the table. As Questioner speaks, the other actors quietly find seats.

QUESTIONER   Human beings! That's us! [*walks over and peers into the mixing bowl*]

But I'm not sure how we're going to fit in there. Before we hear the story of how human beings were put into the Creator's world, we need to pause. Let's take a moment to be grateful for each other, here in this sanctuary. We've been apart for a week, and during that time some of us have had wonderful things happen that are too happy not to share. Some of us may have had very sad or worrisome things happen, that feel like a weight that others can help us carry.

Joys and Sorrows

After the congregation has shared, the Questioner calls for a period of silent meditation and allows at least a minute of silence.

Thank you for sharing from your heart, so that all of our eyes can see the rich, beautiful colors and patterns that live inside us. Let us shift our meditation into music as we remain seated and sing.

"Dear Weaver of Our Lives' Design," *SLT,* 22

Actors resume their places.

STORYTELLER The Creator decided to shake in a sample from among her boxes, labeled "Human Beings."

Universe and Questioner each take a large picture frame and walk up to different people in the congregation, pausing briefly to frame an individual's face, smiling into their eyes, and moving to another person while the Storyteller continues.

She combined people of all sizes and shapes and ages, with many colors of skin and hair, many different kinds of noses, and many different interests and skills. All of it was so beautiful, because each one was different. Over all the people she sprinkled some powder called "Change" so that people would change interests and skills. She sprinkled "Responsibility" so that people would care for the earth and each other.

Creator throws into the air unscented baby powder, confetti, or sparkly fairy dust.

CREATOR That will make this new planet interesting. I'm glad I thought of doing this!

Creator is reflective and then turns to her shelves to prepare the next potion.

STORYTELLER She looked in the section of her closet called "Emotions and Senses," and she wondered whether she should add a little or a lot. She started with "Love" and then she closed her eyes and reached in and took a handful of "Sadness," "Courage," "Loneliness," "Happiness," "Memory," and "Hope."

Creator shakes shakers into bowl while Universe and Questioner make these faces or demonstrate these emotions in body language.

She shook out "Smell," "Touch," "Taste," "Sight," and "Hearing." There was so much beauty for her human beings to see, and hear, and touch. But the smells and tastes were extra-special, and the people loved some of the tastes and smells more than others!

Universe and Questioner pass around the baskets of chocolates. (If the congregation is large, volunteers can help.) The Storyteller allows time for the treats to make their way around as Creator stirs up her planet.

Finally, the Creator was almost done. Almost.

The actors freeze or quietly take their seats once again.

QUESTIONER One of the great gifts of being human is that we're invited to be co-creators, as we nurture the earth and its many gifts. We are invited to care for the mountains, rivers, and fields; we are trusted to care for the creatures of fur, feather, and fins that inhabit the earth. We're called to care for each other as human beings. One way that we continually weave a new creation, as life continues to unfold around us, is to create and sustain institutions that serve us. We build schools for people to learn; we build hospitals where people can go for healing; we build churches and temples to remember what's important in life. Our giving of resources to this congregation is one way that we act as stewards of this institution, and as co-creators of this community. As we gather this morning's offering, I invite you to experience the giving of your money as sweet as the chocolate that you received a few moments ago!

Offering

Actors resume their places.

STORYTELLER   There was one more ingredient the Creator wanted to add. She moved jars around, looking for one special jar she remembered that she had, but had never used before. She carefully lifted down a little jar labeled "Freedom." This time she had to read the label because she didn't remember exactly what was in the jar.

CREATOR   [*reading label*] "This compound contains choice: to choose one thing instead of another. Use cautiously, because the choices made will have consequences." [*smiles and gazes into the bowl*] This will make it especially interesting.

UNIVERSE   Indeed it does!

QUESTIONER   Yup, it suuuuuuure does.

CREATOR   I wonder what freedom will do for these new beings?

Creator acts out the scene that follows, as described by the Storyteller. (The falling tear can be indicated by running a finger down the cheek.)

STORYTELLER   She held the open jar in her hands, slowly turning it as she looked down into it. A soft chuckle rumbled out of her mouth and into the jar. A tear trickled down her cheek and into the jar, also. She leaned over and blew in her warm breath, then poured the freedom into the mix. And then she screwed on the cover and put the jar away. Her new planet was ready to be sent into the star-speckled darkness.

Universe and Questioner move closer to the congregation, extending the parachute or a large swath of fabric between them. Creator takes out a formerly hidden inflatable Earth ball/globe and gently tosses it onto the parachute. Universe and Questioner begin to roll the Earth, gently, between them.

Her new planet landed just where she intended—about 93 million miles from her favorite sun. The Creator watched her planet settle into its new home and waited to see what would happen.

QUESTIONER   As we watch this new planet spin in place, let us remain seated and sing together "For the Earth Forever Turning."

During the hymn, all of the actors, gently and with reverence, roll the Earth ball around on the billowing parachute/cloth.

"For the Earth Forever Turning," *SLT,* 163

As the hymn ends, the actors lay the cloth and Earth on the ground. All of them, except Questioner, take their seats.

QUESTIONER   As we move from our story into a guided meditation, you are invited to wonder why the Creator cried a tear into the earth when she added freedom. You are also welcome to follow your own practice of meditation or prayer. Let's spend a few moments in the quiet of this place, remembering the beauty of our bodies, our minds, and our spirits. After some silence, I will speak some words for guided meditation. [*allows people to meditate in silence for a minute or so*]

Our freedom to choose one thing or another, with consequences, can feel juicy and ripe with possibility. Think of a time when you felt freedom as a blessing, and felt excited about all of the wonderful outcomes that could blossom from that freedom. [*pauses for a moment of silence*]

Allow yourself to remember what it felt like to make a decision with certainty, with confidence. Feel in your heart that sense of happiness, and the promise of growing a bud into a beautiful flower, that came just from your choosing to do something. Remember your wisdom, your power. [*pauses again for silence*]

Sometimes, our freedom to make a choice feels frightening, as if we didn't trust ourselves or were stuck in a situation with no good outcome. Think of a time when freedom felt frightening to you, as if the consequences weren't welcome and you wanted someone else to make a decision for you. [*pauses*]

Remember, in your time of frightening freedom, the people who helped you feel strong and safe—even if it was yourself. Remember those who helped you make that decision, who supported you. Hold in gratitude all of the people who loved you, even if your freedom led you to choose something that had painful consequences. [*pauses*]

Look back with your older, wiser eyes and understand how freedom has been a teacher. Part of your becoming was guided by having freedom. Whether your decisions had happy consequences, or whether freedom has gotten you in trouble, open your heart to understand that freedom has helped you grow and learn. [*pauses*]

Finally, consider where in your life today you see the people you love struggling with decisions, with their freedom. Notice who may be frightened by his or her freedom. In these last moments of meditation, create an intention to help someone find the gift, the juiciness and promise, in their freedom. Create an intention to show someone close to you that no one needs to confront freedom alone; each of us can be a comfort and a voice of wisdom. [*pauses*]

When you are ready, feel your breath moving in your body. Feel the chair, the floor, the earth, holding you. Feel the warmth of the person next to you, and the community filling this room. Look around, and remember what a gift we are to each other. Know that this community will help you celebrate your many freedoms. Know that, when freedom seems frightening, this community will journey with you toward the unknown. May it be so.

"I'm On My Way," *SLT,* 116

QUESTIONER   As we re-enter this world that we call home,
may our eyes be open to the beauty around us
and the beauty inside each person.
May we remember the gift of freedom—
in all of its frightening, juicy privilege—
and may we use our freedom to make bold,
    confident choices
to deepen love and justice in the world.

The Right Way to Right Speech

Have you ever received advice that you didn't want? How do you know if you're truly being helpful when you try to help someone? This service tells the story of Motke the fish peddler, who was helped a little too much by his friends. The story, based on Simms Taback's version of a Jewish folk tale, leads into an exploration of the Buddhist concept of "right speech," in which we ask what we can do, in our congregations, to communicate in better and healthier ways.

Preparation (moderate)

- Create many fake fish—1 or 2 dozen, or more. One way to make a fake fish is to cut out 2 large fish-shaped pieces of paper, stuff wadded paper between them, and staple them together.
- Make large cards with Velcro on the back, one for each word in the phrase "Fresh Fish Sold Here Daily." Prepare a piece of foam-core with corresponding Velcro pieces (so that the pieces are removable), and attach the cards to the foam-core in the correct order.
- Obtain a pushcart or wagon or find another way for Motke to transport his fish.
- Obtain a small table or stand to serve as Motke's "fish stall" and tuck it somewhere off-stage.
- Draw the outline of a fish on half-sheets of paper and insert one into each order of service.
- Fill several baskets with pens and pencils.

- Check with your congregation's leadership to make sure it's okay to hang in a public place all the fish used in the service.
- Have Motke and the Kibitzers seated in the front row of the sanctuary
- *Rehearsal will take between 2 and 3 hours.*

Roles   (9 or 11, those who need to attend rehearsal are marked with *)

- Leader* (can also serve as the Storyteller)
- Storyteller*
- Motke*
- 6 Kibitzers
- 2 Sign-holders (Optional. Instead of Motke hanging his sign in a spot visible to the congregation, two tall people can hold it high above his fish stand.) (Called "Holders" in the script.)

Welcome

The Leader welcomes congregants.

LEADER   As we begin our worship service for all ages, let us join in singing our centering hymn, "Spirit of Life."

"Spirit of Life," *SLT*, 123

Chalice Lighting

STORYTELLER   Have you ever received unwelcome advice? Have you ever been doing something well, or reasonably well, or maybe not very well at all but at least perfectly happily, only to have someone else tell you all the ways that you were doing it wrong? Have you ever been helped a little too "helpfully" by someone when you didn't really want their help? You're not alone—that's how Motke felt.

Motke stands and waves to the congregation, then sits back down.

Who's Motke? Well, "Motke" is a nickname for boys or men who are named Mordecai. Today we're going to hear a story about a fish peddler named Motke Rabinowitz. The story was written by a man named Simms Taback. Simms heard this story, once upon a time, from his zayda, his Grandpa—in fact, his zayda told him a lot of stories when Simms was a boy. Simms' zayda, and his zayda's stories, come from the Jewish tradition. Those stories have some Yiddish words in them. Do you know what Yiddish is? You've already learned one Yiddish word: zayda means "Grandpa"! You may know even more Yiddish than that, though. Do you know what a klutz is? [allows a volunteer to define "klutz"]

Have you ever heard of chutzpah? [lets someone explain what chutzpah is]

Have you ever said "yada yada yada" when someone was talking too much? Well, that's Yiddish! Almost all of us speak a little bit of Yiddish, even though we may not know it. Many Yiddish words have become part of everyday English. Yiddish is part of this story about Motke Rabinowitz the fish peddler, because this story is full of kibitzers and cockamamie! That's more Yiddish. A kibitzer thinks she knows better than you. A kibitzer gives advice that's not very good and that nobody asked for in the first place. A kibitzer is always sticking his nose in other people's business. You may be wondering: So, what is Yiddish? Simms Taback thinks of Yiddish as a big pot of soup with a little of this and a little of that thrown in: German dialect mixed with a little French and a little Italian. Yiddish was once the everyday language of the Jewish people who lived in Eastern Europe. Their lives were sometimes difficult, but they struggled on, and found strength in their songs, their dances, and most of all, their stories—just like the stories that Simms Taback heard from his zayda. As we enter into worship, we'll join in singing words that are similar to Yiddish: the Hebrew words of the hymn, "Shalom Havayreem," which mean "Peace, my friends; Peace, my friends; Peace, peace; Until we meet again; Until we meet again; Peace, peace."

"**Shalom Havayreem**," *SLT,* 400

STORYTELLER   We finished singing just in time. Here comes Motke the fish peddler now!

Motke pulls his cart or wagon full of fish to the center of the chancel and acts out the story as the Storyteller continues.

Motke was a fish peddler—which means that he would go out in his boat early in the morning, catch some fish, and then take them around from house to house on his old pushcart, selling them from door to door. By afternoon, he usually had sold all of his fish—all but one, which he would take home and cook up as a tasty supper. Motke was an excellent fisherman, and as he propelled his heavy pushcart through the streets, he often found himself wishing that he could sell his fish in a way that would be easier on his poor, aching back. One day, Motke had an idea: Why not sell his pushcart and rent a storefront? How easy it would be to sell his catch of fish then!

Motke pulls out his fish stall from off-stage, transferring fish onto it from his cart or wagon.

So that's exactly what Motke did: He looked around the little town, found an excellent spot for his fish stand, and began to set up shop. Noticing the other shops near his fish stall, however, he realized that people might not see his fish stand in the middle of so many other things for sale.

MOTKE   Why not do a little advertising? I need a sign. Let's see ... shall I paint "Rabinowitz" on it? Nah ... not everyone knows that I'm the fish peddler. What about ... hmmm ...

STORYTELLER   Motke needs some help, I think. Do you have any ideas about what Motke Rabinowitz could put on his sign for his store? [*allows congregation to call out their marketing ideas*]

Those are all great ideas. Here's what Motke did: After thinking about it long and hard, Motke painted a sign to hang over the doorway of his little store, with these words:

Motke pulls out his sign and places it in a spot visible to the entire congregation.

OR: Two Sign-holders enter scene and hold sign high over Motke's stand.

MOTKE [*reading sign*] Fresh Fish Sold Here Daily.

In the following scenes, each Kibitzer stands and enters scene, as prompted by the Storyteller's description. After delivering line(s), each Kibitzer returns to their seat.

STORYTELLER Motke had just climbed a ladder, hung the sign, climbed back down, and put the ladder away when his first customer arrived. He began to sell his catch for the day. Among the stream of customers, a kibitzer passed by.

KIBITZER 1 What kind of cockamamie sign is that?

MOTKE Why? What's wrong with it?

KIBITZER 1 Fresh Fish Sold Here Daily? Fresh? Why say "Fresh Fish"? Of course it's fresh! Would you sell fish that wasn't fresh? Your customers may get suspicious, no?

MOTKE Yes! I mean, no! You're absolutely right.

STORYTELLER So Motke painted out the word "Fresh" and replaced the sign, settling back behind his counter of fish. His sign now read:

Motke removes the card that says "Fresh" from his sign.

MOTKE [*reading sign*] Fish Sold Here Daily.

STORYTELLER Motke went out the next morning to fish, and as he carried his catch to his tiny store, he gazed up at his sign proudly. It didn't look half-bad, with the "Fresh" removed. As his customers arrived, he forgot all about the sign until a second kibitzer came by.

KIBITZER 2 I like your sign, Motke.

MOTKE Thank you.

KIBITZER 2   But should you say "Sold"? Of course you sell fish. This is a store, no? Every merchant here is selling their goods, no? You don't give your fish away for free! Do you really need to tell people you're selling the fish?

MOTKE   Yes! I mean, no. I mean, of course!

STORYTELLER   Once again, Motke climbed up to his sign and painted out the word "Sold."

Motke removes the card that says "Sold" from his sign.

Now Motke's sign said:

MOTKE   [*reading sign*] Fish Here Daily.

STORYTELLER   As he looked at the twice-altered sign, Motke thought that keeping three words out of the original five wasn't so bad. It was short and to the point. Yes, he nodded to himself, the sign was much better now. As the morning turned to afternoon, Motke sold a number of his fish to the women and cooks in the village. He began to feel quite satisfied that this sign of his was drawing many customers . . . until a third kibitzer came by. As before, Motke received a compliment on his handsome sign first. Eventually, however, the kibitzer quizzed him.

KIBITZER 3   Say, Rabinowitz, why do you say "Here" on the sign? Fish Here Daily? Are you selling fish somewhere else, too? Where else would you be, if not here?

MOTKE   Yes! I mean, no! You're right!

STORYTELLER   So Motke painted out "Here."

Motke removes the card that says "Here" from his sign.

Now Motke's sign said:

MOTKE   [*reading sign*] Fish Daily.

STORYTELLER   As he packed up his little storefront for the day, and wrapped up his fish to take home for supper, Motke felt slightly puzzled. He couldn't quite remember how his magnificent, five-word sign had now been reduced to the words "Fish" and "Daily."

Motke (and, if applicable, Sign-holders) sit down.

LEADER One way that we build our community and make each other strong is not by calling each other "cockamamie" and "klutz," but instead by using kind and compassionate words to speak to one another. Sharing our joys and sorrows is not about calling names and giving advice! Rather, it's a way to enter into a relationship of kindness: When we share the special or sad moments in our lives, and invite people to see into our hearts, then we're also asking for their support. We're letting them know that, outside of worship—whether it's at coffee hour or over the phone during the week—we need them to offer their friendship and strength and listening ears.

Joys and Sorrows

After the congregation has shared, the Leader calls for a period of silent meditation and allows at least a minute of silence.

LEADER Great Mystery, Web of Life and of Love,
We give thanks for this caring community of all ages and colors,
this group of people who hold our sadness when it overflows
    in us,
and share our joy in the same way.

We're grateful for the gift of speech,
that we might offer our creativity and help,
and speak of our love and commitment to each other.

We're grateful for the gift of listening,
through which we invite the speech of others,
opening their hearts to unlock wisdom and healing.

We're grateful for the gift of reflection,
with which we discern when to speak,
when to listen,
and when to simply *be* in each other's presence.

As we sit in your Presence,
may we renew our commitment to use these gifts carefully,
both within and beyond these walls.

Please join me as we continue to meditate through singing.

"Though I May Speak with Bravest Fire," *SLT*, 34

Motke and, if applicable, Sign-holders with sign, return.

STORYTELLER   The next day, like every other day, Motke again carried his catch of fish to his little store with its thrice-altered sign. He had just sold a handful of herring to a neighbor when he spotted another kibitzer approaching.

KIBITZER 4   Hey Rabinowitz! Your sign is a little farblondjet.

STORYTELLER   Farblondjet is a Yiddish word that means "confused."

KIBITZER 4   [*reads*] Fish Daily. Fish daily? What do you mean by "Daily"? If fish are fresh, they don't come in and go out weekly, do they? And your fish are fresh, are they not?

MOTKE   Yes! I mean, no! I'm in complete agreement!

STORYTELLER   After all, Motke reasoned to himself, he went out in his boat every single day, and the whole village knew it. Perhaps there was no point in taking up space on his sign with that bit of unnecessary information. And so Motke took down the sign, as he had done three times already, and painted out the word "Daily."

Motke removes the card with the word "Daily" from his sign.

Now Motke's sign said only:

MOTKE   [*reading sign*] Fish.

STORYTELLER   Motke was looking up at the sign, reckoning with his growing suspicion that something now looked . . . funny . . . about the sign. The kibitzer had called the sign farblondjet—

confused—but that's exactly how Motke was starting to feel! Suddenly, a fifth kibitzer strolled by.

KIBITZER 5   Pardon me, Rabinowitz. I don't mean to butt in. But why are you putting up a useless sign that says "Fish" when you can smell your fish a mile away?

STORYTELLER   Why indeed, thought Rabinowitz ruefully. So Motke the fish peddler took down the sign altogether. How fortunate he was to get such good advice, he thought! How helpful his neighbors were! What luck that he had others to guide him in his fish-peddling efforts!

Motke and the Storyteller relax, as if to end there.

[*suddenly*] But that's not the end of the story. The next day, Motke was sitting in his tiny fish stall, patiently waiting for the day's customers. Another kibitzer came by—a man who hadn't had a chance to see Motke's beautiful, fleeting, shrinking sign.

KIBITZER 6   Rabinowitz, it looks like you don't have any customers.

MOTKE   Well, for the past few mornings, I've had brisk sales. But this morning, eh, business is a little slow.

STORYTELLER   And the kibitzer asked . . .

KIBITZER 6   So why don't you hang out a sign?

Motke and the other actors take their seats.

LEADER   Ah, how easy it is to give suggestions, advice, and ideas to other people! It's a little bit harder to put ourselves in other people's shoes, listen to them carefully, and then offer useful help. In order to make a meaningful contribution, you need to care about the outcome. Our support of this congregation works like that, too. Each week, we take an offering to sustain the work of this [church/fellowship], both inside our walls and beyond them. We care about growing this congregation into the future, and that caring requires that we give in thoughtful, substantial ways. As we collect this morning's offering, please know how valuable your contribution is, and how deeply we appreciate your many ways of giving.

Offering

STORYTELLER Do you remember what the Yiddish word kibitzer means? [*allows someone to offer the definition*]

When our service began this morning, I explained that a kibitzer thinks he knows better than you do. A kibitzer gives advice that's not very good and that nobody asked for in the first place. A kibitzer is always sticking her nose in other people's business. In our story about Motke Rabinowitz the fish peddler, so many kibitzers gave advice to Motke that his sign became less and less sensible. The kibitzers gave advice that Motke never asked for and wasn't very good—that's a bad combination! Maybe the kibitzers were trying to help Motke, but they only ended up confusing things.

LEADER Sometimes, we're a little like kibitzers: We think we know the answer to someone else's problems, or we suggest what they should do before they've asked us, or we give advice only when it's too late. Can you think of a time when you did any of these things? [*asks for a show of hands from people who can admit to having ever given unsolicited or too-late advice*]

There's another religious tradition—Buddhism—that has something to teach us about when to speak and when to keep silent. In the Buddhist tradition, "right speech" means knowing how and when to use our words. You can probably guess what right speech is, since all of us know something about when communication feels right and when it feels . . . well, not right. In the Buddhist tradition, the definition of right speech differs slightly from teacher to teacher, but there are four conditions that most Buddhists agree on. Do you want to guess the characteristics of right speech? [*takes guesses from the congregation*]

STORYTELLER According to Buddhist teachers, right speech entails these things: first, our words need to be truthful.

LEADER   That's pretty easy. Most of us know when we're saying something that's true, and when we're saying something that's not true.

STORYTELLER   Second, right speech is speech that's kind, and that promotes harmony. As our song puts it, we can speak with "bravest fire," but if our words don't have love, then our voices are like "sounding brass"—clanging cymbals. All of us know how important love is, because everyone here has probably been on the receiving end of words that hurt your feelings or made you feel put down. Words matter; there are many ways to phrase a single message. Kind speech happens when we make the effort to find words that leave the other person feeling good.

LEADER   So far, right speech seems pretty simple, doesn't it? If you can be kind and can say what's true, that's a lot of leeway. Let's learn the other half of right speech to see if things stay so simple!

STORYTELLER   The third part of right speech is that we speak in a timely manner. "Timely" means that we speak up in the moment, when people are actively trying to solve the problem—not later, when the problem is worse and it's too late for our insight to help.

LEADER   I think I get it. You mean, if I accidentally break something, I should tell someone right away, and not wait for them to find it a few days later?

STORYTELLER   Exactly. And there's only one more thing to add, the fourth part: Our words become right speech when they're helpful, or useful. We speak when there's a reasonable chance of our words being beneficial to another person—when that person really needs to know something that we know, and wants our input to change something. But don't forget about kindness! Sometimes we give advice that makes us look good, but puts the other person down. Speech that is truly useful makes the other person—and the relationship between us—stronger.

LEADER   What does that have to do with Motke trying to sell fish?

STORYTELLER   [*addresses one of the six Kibitzers, who are all sitting in the front row*] You probably thought you were just being honest when you advised Motke on his sign, right? [*gently addresses another Kibitzer from the story*] And you—you were timely in your advice, because you sure didn't waste any time giving Motke your honest opinion. [*addresses all Kibitzers*] In fact, all of you may have been trying to be helpful, but . . . Motke, did you feel like you were receiving kind, helpful feedback?

MOTKE   [*stands, speaks to Kibitzers*] Not exactly.

Kibitzers turn to Motke and hug him, perhaps apologizing.

LEADER   Does right speech remind you of anything? Does it remind you of anything that we do here in this Unitarian Universalist congregation? Here's a hint: it's another two-word phrase that begins with the word "right." [*waits for someone to come up with the term "right relationship"*]

Right relationship! Right relationship is important in our Unitarian Universalist congregations. Here's why: We Unitarian Universalists don't all have to believe the same things, but we do share what's called a covenant—a solemn promise—to care for each other. We show our care and love for each other by treating each other with respect, but also by communicating well. And some Unitarian Universalists call that "right relationship."

Volunteers pass out pens.

Before we leave this service, we're each going to go fishing! Instead of fishing for fish, we're fishing for words that lead to right relationship, to loving covenant. Inside your order of service there's a fish—not a real one, of course—that's Motke's territory.

Take a moment, now, to reflect on this question: What words, coming from another member of this congregation, have warmed your heart? What words have made you feel valued and cherished? For you kids, here's another way to think of it: Imagine a time when you felt sad or lonely. What did someone say to make you feel loved? When you're ready, write on your fish the words that symbolize right speech or right relationship to you. If there's someone next to you who needs help writing, please help them, too. [*allows a few minutes for this to happen*]

So that we can learn how to make each other feel cared for and valued, all of your fish are going to be hung so that we can read each others' wishes for right speech here in this congregation. Please make sure that you [*tape/hang*] your fish up on your way out this morning. [*If there's time remaining in the service, the Leader can ask people to volunteer to stand and read what they've written.*]

As we end this service of friendship and fun and go into our day, and into the coming week, let's remember that making our communication feel good is an important way to show that we care for one another . . . whether we're here, or out selling fish!

"Love Will Guide Us," *SLT,* 131

LEADER   May love guide us, from sunrise on into the night.
May hope inside us lead the way to that love.
May the words from our mouths,
the meditations of our hearts,
and the work of our hands
make visible our love for each other,
our community, and our world.

After the service, hang the congregation's fish on the sanctuary wall or in a fishnet that's hung in a public space.

Strong Is What We Make Each Other

In this story, Monkey and Hare work themselves into a disagreement by blustering through misunderstanding instead of sharing what's in their hearts. Hare offers Monkey a sassy challenge, and then he gets stumped as to how to win it. In this worship service, we sing, drum, and hear the story about Monkey and Hare's contest to build the best hut. The lesson is that living together in community is the greatest gift we have to give and receive. This service is adapted from the story "Hare's Gifts" by Rev. Ken Collier.

Preparation (significant)

- Ask people to bring canned goods to the service for a local food pantry or community organization.

- Print the words to all 5 sung refrains in the order of service. They are:

    Refrain #1
    For such beauty we are thankful. For such beauty we are thankful.
    For such beauty we are thankful. Praises to this world.

    Refrain #2
    In our circle, who is inside? In our circle, who is outside?
    Let us make our circle larger, sisters, brothers, all.

    Refrain #3
    If I stumble, will you help me? If I stumble, will you help me?
    If I stumble, will you help me? Will you hear my cry?

Refrain #4
On and on the circle's moving. On and on the circle's moving.
On and on the circle's moving, sisters, brothers, all.

Refrain #5
Strong is what we make each other. Strong is what we make
    each other.
Strong is what we make each other, sisters, brothers, all.

- Create simple costumes for Monkey and Hare or obtain monkey and hare puppets.

- Make 2 huts from folding screens, tents, or card tables (one of these will be Monkey's new hut; the other, Hare's old hut).

- Find an old rickety umbrella for Monkey's old hut.

- Find something to stand for a baobab pod. Technically, a baobab pod is the size and shape of a miniature football, but anything safe to throw will work fine.

- Gather miscellaneous tools for building Hare's new hut; a drum for Hare to play; and simple percussion instruments, such as shakers, for the extras.

- *Rehearsal will take between 2 and 3 hours.*

Roles (6–8, all should attend rehearsal)
- Storyteller
- Leader
- Monkey
- Hare
- 2–4 Extras (non-speaking roles)

Note: This service ends with Hare drumming. If you need to, change the drum to another instrument and slightly alter the script. Keep this musical need in mind when you cast the role of Hare, or prepare to have a hidden drummer doing the actual playing.

As the service begins, the Storyteller and the Leader are at the front of the sanctuary. One hut is in place.

STORYTELLER Many years ago, before we were born, before our grandmothers and grandfathers were born, and before our grandmothers' grandmothers were born, no one lived in towns or villages. Instead, everyone just set up a hut any old place. It was a trifle inconvenient, but it never occurred to anyone to live in any other way. No one noticed that having people's huts scattered here and there made things a little lonely. All of that changed when Hare built his hut.

Hare enters and, as the Storyteller continues, nestles in his hut.

Hare lived in a corner of the world far away from where we live today, over mountains and oceans and treetops, on the edge of a forest. Monkey also lived there; these two creatures had put their huts near each other under the shadow of the forest. Hare was happy with his small but comfortable hut. It gave him a cozy place to sleep at night, and a place to eat his greens when he got hungry.

Monkey appears with the old umbrella for her "hut," and opens it, sulking.

Monkey's hut was the same size as Hare's, but Monkey was not happy with her hut. She thought that it was too crowded, and not very pretty. Monkey's hut had cracks in the roof that let the baobab pods and fireflies in. Of course, baobab pods and fireflies are both lovely, so it's not a bother to have them in one's hut. But that's how Monkey was: a little grouchy and a little gruff.

Hare and Monkey exit.

Welcome

The Leader thanks the Storyteller and welcomes congregants and visitors.

LEADER Like Monkey, maybe you woke up on the wrong side of the bed, and feel a little grouchy and a little gruff. We welcome you, however you're feeling, and hope that our multigenerational service brightens your spirits. Our worship leaders and I share our gifts with you this morning in the spirit of celebration and playfulness, but this story also comes to you in the spirit of "worship"—worth shape—giving shape to the things that have worth to us as a religious community. The wisdom in the story of Hare and Monkey is just one shape, one form, of our shared values.

Chalice Lighting

We light our chalice this morning for the beauty of the earth:
For fireflies, bright lilies and the sparkling sunlight,
the hills and mountains, and the moon that rises above the horizon.
We light this chalice for the beauty of this company,
these familiar faces and new friends,
and the hands that form an ever-expanding circle of joy, love, and peace.

LEADER Throughout today's service, we will sing refrains to the tune of "We Are Climbing Jacob's Ladder." Please sing with me the first sung response, printed in your order of service:

Note: The tune to this and all sung responses in this service is found in SLT, 211.

For such beauty we are thankful. For such beauty we are thankful. For such beauty we are thankful. Praises to this world.

Hare sits in her hut, watching, as Monkey acts out the following story as it is told.

STORYTELLER One day, Monkey was sitting in her hut, thinking grumpily about how small it was. She didn't mind the plain walls or the dirt floor, but it did feel quite small. She was so busy thinking these grumpy thoughts that she never noticed that one of the cracks in the hut's roof had turned into a sizeable hole. She didn't notice that she was sitting right under it . . . and she certainly didn't notice that there was a grand and heavy baobab branch right over the hole. Suddenly, a strong breeze came along, knocking a big baobab pod through the hole in the roof and—thump!—it fell right on Monkey's head.

The Storyteller gently tosses the pod at Monkey.

MONKEY   That does it!

STORYTELLER   The pod that thumped Monkey on the head was the straw that broke the camel's back. Monkey decided then and there to set up a new hut that would be the biggest and grandest ever made—with a sturdy roof, to boot. She searched out a good site near sweet water and in the cool shade of an enormous baobab tree and set out to build the strong-roofed hut.

Monkey closes her umbrella, tosses it aside, and sets up her new hut.

In time it was finished, and it was indeed grand. It was enormously tall and its walls were white and bright and decorated with the most wonderful designs: zigzags and spirals and circles. Monkey was proud of her new hut and decided to have a feast to show it off. She went around to all the other huts and invited everyone—even Hare.

A few Extras come to admire the hut and celebrate with Monkey. Hare exits scene.

And everyone came and admired Monkey's hut and then stayed to have a good time—everyone, that is, except Hare, who didn't come at all.

LEADER   Please join in singing our second shared response:
In our circle, who is inside? In our circle, who is outside?
Let us make our circle larger, sisters, brothers, all.

Extras exit. Hare enters scene, settling in his hut. Monkey and Hare act out the following scene as it is described.

STORYTELLER   The next day Monkey, who was insulted by Hare not coming to the feast, went to him and angrily demanded to know why he hadn't come to admire the grand new hut. The truth was, Hare had forgotten all about Monkey's feast—he'd been sidetracked by a patch of juicy berries on the other side of the mountain. It was only when he returned home that he remembered the event. But Hare was too embarrassed to admit this, and thoughtlessly tried to bluster his way out of Monkey's confrontation.

HARE Grand new hut! Bah! Why should I come to see your hut? I could build a better one in half the time. And as for your feast, why should I come to your feast and be bored? I could give a feast that would make everyone forget yours.

STORYTELLER Monkey's feelings were hurt by Hare's words, but she didn't say so. Part of her wanted to be tough, and to give Hare a hard time. So Monkey stepped back with a smug smile.

MONKEY [*steps back, scoffing, incredulous, with a smug smile*] A better hut? In half the time? I don't think so. It took me a full moon to build and decorate my hut. And how could you give a feast better than mine? You don't even have opposable thumbs! If a challenge is what you want, a challenge you shall have: I dare you to build a new hut in half a moon. Afterwards, your feast had better be a good one. If you fail to do either of these things, perhaps my winter robe will be made of . . . Hare skin!

STORYTELLER Monkey left, feeling terrible about the mean things she said to Hare, and still hurt that Hare hadn't come to celebrate her new hut. She wondered how Hare would be able to build his hut. She didn't want a winter robe of Hare skin! She went back to her grand new hut, feeling uneasy and very lonely. But Hare had taken Monkey's threat to heart and was worried.

Monkey exits.

HARE [*scratches head, says to self*] You've really done it this time, Hare. When will you learn to keep your big mouth shut? And why didn't I just go to the feast, to celebrate Monkey's new hut? I suppose I was jealous, but now I'm really in a pickle.

STORYTELLER And Hare sat down to think about what on earth he was going to do.

LEADER Just like Monkey and Hare, sometimes we say things that we don't mean. Like Monkey, we allow our hurt feelings to turn into harsh words. Like Hare, we don't see how much other people need us to be kind to them. We forget that it's important to tell our friends and neighbors how we're feeling, and to listen to what they say back to us. Our sharing of joys and sorrows is important because it allows us to stop, every week, and show the soft side of our hearts. It helps us remember that everybody—even gruff, grumpy people—feel sad sometimes. We listen to remember that the joys and sorrows in life are sometimes woven together so closely that there's no separation. If there's a happy celebration in your life, or a sad weight in your heart, this is the time to come forward and say a few words about it.

Joys and Sorrows

After the congregation has shared, the Leader calls for a period of silent meditation and allows at least a minute of silence.

LEADER Spirit of the baobab trees and butterflies,
Spirit that blows down from the mountain and burns up through the fire,
we give thanks for the people in this sanctuary.
They have strong arms to hold us when we need a hug.
They have a steady presence when our lives are shaken.
They remind us to be wise with our words, generous with our actions,
and thankful for the gifts in our lives.
May we each become the person we want to be,
and in so doing may we, as a loving people,
become the congregation we want to become.

Please sing our third meditation with me:

If I stumble, will you help me? If I stumble, will you help me?
If I stumble, will you help me? Will you hear my cry?

STORYTELLER   Hare was still stumped as to how to get out of his predicament: he had too much pride to patch things up with Monkey, so it seemed his only option was to build a hut more beautiful than hers—and in half a moon! Hare wasn't strong enough to build a hut by himself. He did not have enough ginger root stored up to trade with others for their labor. What could he do? Do you have any ideas?

HARE   [*to the congregation*] Help me! What do you think I should do? [*listens to responses from the congregation*]

STORYTELLER   Well, this is what happened: Suddenly Hare jumped up and ran to all of the other huts scattered across the land to ask everyone to come and help him. To get them to come, he promised everyone two marvelous, unheard-of gifts and a wonderful feast when all the work was finished. All they had to do was come live near him, and help him for half a moon.

The Extras come to the area where Hare's new hut will be, and act out the following scene, erecting the second hut.

   The others arrived, one family at a time, and Hare was flooded with gratitude. He thanked them, and showed them where to set up their huts. When everyone had arrived, they set to work. Hare talked to every person to find out what they each did best. The best woodworkers found, straightened, and set the poles; the best painters mixed and painted the walls; the best artists set to decorating them; and all the others began to prepare the food and drink for the feast. All of the helpers were so busy that they didn't quite notice that Hare had managed to get everyone else to do all the work. That is, he wasn't straightening or setting poles. He wasn't painting. He wasn't even preparing food for the feast (he planned to visit that lovely berry patch to pick enough berries for all of the helpers, just not right now). Instead, Hare was doing something completely different: he carefully searched around the woods and found a hollow log and a couple of sticks. And then he spent the entire half moon carving out the log. What could he be planning?

LEADER   Trusting that some great project will emerge from the mystery, please join in our fourth sung response.

On and on the circle's moving. On and on the circle's moving. On and on the circle's moving, sisters, brothers, all.

Monkey approaches the other actors and acts out the following scene as the Storyteller describes it.

STORYTELLER   By the end of the half moon, Monkey was wondering what she would find when she went to see Hare and his new hut. She had concluded that she would encounter Hare in a mess of construction, with no hut to show off. It's not that she wanted Hare to fail; she just couldn't possibly imagine how he would meet her challenge. As Monkey rounded the bend of the river, she was amazed to see something . . . not at all what she'd expected. Hare had a new hut! There it was, shining in the sun.

MONKEY   [*disguising that she is impressed*] Hmph. That's some hut you've got there. Not bad, Hare. Tell me, though: just how is this better than my hut?

HARE   Just look around, and you'll see!

STORYTELLER   As Monkey looked around, she realized that Hare's hut wasn't alone. Arrayed around his hut were more huts, arranged in a circle, all facing east, to the rising sun. They were the huts of all those who had come to help Hare, and who had stayed. There the others were, going about their business, laughing and talking and helping each other.

The others' huts can be imaginary.

HARE   My hut is better than yours because it was built by everyone. Even better, everyone lives near it, so we can continue to have fun together.

STORYTELLER   The others, who heard all of this, looked around and realized that it really was sweet to live together. They could share tasks, each doing what they were best at. They could help one another. Knowing one another so well meant that they could trust one another to care for them. They didn't have to live scattered apart from one another and feel lonely! They could be a community! And that was Hare's first gift, which he had promised: the gift of the village.

LEADER Remembering the gift of our own community, let us sing together our final sung response:

Strong is what we make each other. Strong is what we make each other.
Strong is what we make each other, sisters, brothers, all.

Like those who helped Hare build his hut, we need to remember to stop and look around our own community once in a while. Take a good look around right now, and see the people you've helped, the people you've learned with, broken bread with, and shared with. It really is sweet to live together, and it really is a gift to make a village of our congregation, where we make each other strong. This isn't just one of Hare's gifts; it's a gift that we've all received. As we gather this morning's offering, allow your joy for this community to deepen your level of giving back to this congregation. We will now collect the offering.

Offering

STORYTELLER When Monkey saw that Hare had indeed built a better hut than hers, she lost her smile. Secretly, she was relieved that she wouldn't have to follow through on her mean words about a winter robe of Hare skin! She was also impressed by the village that had emerged out of the work, and a little envious. She didn't know whether there would be room for her in the village, and she realized that no matter how grand her own new hut was, it would be lonely to return to at the end of the day. Still confused about her feelings, Monkey just said:

MONKEY Hmph! Well . . . you also promised a feast better than mine.

STORYTELLER   At the mention of food, everyone ran to get the food and drink they had prepared. In fact, you may have brought food with you this morning, too! If you have any food to share, please bring it forward now ... or have a child bring it to the front. [*allows time for this to happen*]

There was lots and lots of food for Hare and his community to feast on! And because no one had to do it all, each could contribute what he or she cooked best, so the feast had everyone's favorite foods. And that made everyone happy, which, of course, let the storytellers relax and tell their best stories. As all the villagers ate, they offered some food to Monkey. She was surprised at first, but then began to relax when she saw that the others just wanted her to feel welcome, and wanted to share with her.

MONKEY   [*accepting food shyly*] Thank you. Thank you very much.

STORYTELLER   And so Monkey stayed with the new village as the sun dropped from high in the sky to just below the treetops—that's how long the gathering lingered over stories and fine foods. Suddenly, Hare remembered that he had promised a second gift to his new village—but he'd forgotten to bring it out. He slipped away and then came out of his new hut dragging his hollow log.

HARE   You've all been such generous helpers, and I can't thank you enough. Thank you for your work and your companionship. Together we've created a pretty good feast, but I want to make it the best feast ever. It's also time for my second gift. Listen.

Hare (or a hidden drummer) supplies the background music for the following scene. All actors dance and act out the scene that is described.

STORYTELLER   With that, Hare picked up his hollow log and sticks and began to tap on the log with the sticks. At first he beat out a simple beat, and then he warmed up to more and more complex rhythms. Soon the listeners began to twitch with the rhythm and sway and move. Others found logs and empty baobab pods, and joined Hare in his rhythms. Suddenly Monkey realized that she was being included in this new community, and there was no question that she belonged there, with them. Filled with happiness, she jumped up and began to swing her body and move in a circle around the fire, and before long everyone joined her. They danced to the rhythm of the drum Hare had invented and given to them, and to the music that arose from that rhythm.

LEADER We can't let this little village dance by themselves, folks! Please stand, if you're willing and able, and let's clap and dance our way through our final hymn, "This Little Light of Mine."

"This Little Light of Mine," *SLT*, 118.

STORYTELLER Now sometimes folks argue about all of this. Some say that Hare really gave the people three gifts—the village, the drum, and music—while others claim that the music and drum are really only one. Perhaps the gift was that grouchy and gruff Monkey discovered that she could be one of the village. Perhaps the real gift was that both Monkey and Hare realized how important it is to think before speaking, and to be willing to share their feelings instead of blustering through. But you know what I think? I think that when there's a happy ending, counting Hare's gifts hardly matters . . . though I'm sure Hare enjoys the argument.

LEADER May we be mindful of the many gifts that come
   into our lives,
in all their forms, and give thanks for them.
But may we also choose to believe that our greatest gift is found not in what others give us, but in what we share with others.
Go in peace.

Outlawing Jelly Beans, and Other Injustices

How do we use our power? How do we respond to injustice? In this service, based on the story "The Duke Who Outlawed Jelly Beans" by Johnny Valentine, a pompous and power-hungry duke is gently put in his place by the people in his kingdom. When we use our shared power in the name of love, we can overcome almost any obstacle.

Preparation (moderate)

- Notify the congregation that a food offering will be received this Sunday, to provide canned goods for a local food bank.

- Obtain 2 crowns; 2 suitcases; a trumpet, bugle, or kazoo for the Herald (real or toy); a large scroll of paper; and a tabloid magazine.

- Set up a "balcony" or other prominent area from which the Duke will make his proclamations. If your sanctuary has a pulpit, that's the perfect place. Reserve seats for actors playing Beatrice, Emmylou, and Sally in the front of the sanctuary.

- Before the service, ask a few children if they'd like to be part of the story. Have them sit together, near the front, so they can be part of the scene when children huddle with Beatrice and Dexter. If any of the children want a speaking role, you could give them the lines for Extras 1, 2, and 3.

- Provide bowls of jelly beans at coffee hour.

- *Rehearsal will take between 2 and 3 hours.*

Roles (14, those who need to attend rehearsal are marked with *)

- Storyteller* (can also play Herald)
- Leader*
- King
- Queen
- Herald*
- Grand Duke Dwayne* (called "Duke" in the script)
- Beatrice*
- Emmylou*
- Sally*
- Man
- Dexter *
- 3 Extras
- Guard

As the service begins, the Storyteller and the Leader stand at the front of the sanctuary, with the balcony in place behind them.

STORYTELLER   Once there was a royal kingdom, far away, in a land with no rush-hour traffic, infomercials, or email. The kingdom was ruled by a king and queen who enjoyed their work, but felt overwhelmed by the demands of ruling a sizeable kingdom. They consulted with a travel agent, who got them a great deal on a two-week all-inclusive vacation to DragonLand. The king and queen packed their bags and called their subjects for a royal proclamation.

Herald plays (or pretends to play) a trumpet fanfare. King and Queen enter with suitcases.

KING   Hear ye, hear ye! The Queen and I are going on a vacation to frolic and make merry. While we are away, our nephew, the Grand Duke Dwayne, will rule the kingdom. We'll try to send a postcard. See you in two weeks!

STORYTELLER   With that, the king and queen climbed into their coach and pulled away. Immediately the Grand Duke Dwayne strode out onto the castle balcony.

King and Queen exit and Grand Duke Dwayne steps onto the balcony.

DUKE   Hear ye, hear ye . . .

STORYTELLER   Forgive me, Duke, I'm sorry to interrupt. I want to make sure that everyone here feels welcome. Would you mind holding off on your proclamation for a moment while our worship leader does her thing?

Grand Duke Dwayne pouts and sits down, indicating that the Leader may speak.

LEADER   Thanks for waiting, Grand Duke Dwayne.

Welcome

The Leader welcomes congregants and visitors.

LEADER   As you can see, our worship service is a bit different today. Our children will remain present for the entire service, which is woven around a story filled with interesting characters. You've already met the king and queen of the kingdom, and their, ah, colorful nephew, the Grand Duke Dwayne.

As we continue to worship, let us join in singing our opening hymn, "Enter, Rejoice, and Come In." Please stand in body or in spirit.

"Enter, Rejoice, and Come In," *SLT,* 361.

Chalice Lighting

LEADER   Thank you for holding off on your proclamation, Duke. We're interested to hear what you're going to say, so . . . back to you, Storyteller.

Beatrice, Emmylou, and Sally come up front and stand or sit near the balcony.

STORYTELLER   As the Grand Duke Dwayne stood on the balcony, from which his uncle had so recently bid farewell to his subjects, the duke took a deep breath and pronounced arrogantly. . . .

DUKE I have a decree to issue. [*pauses; scratches head*]

Herald plays fanfare, followed by a long pause.

STORYTELLER [*aside, in a loud whisper*] The Duke is a slow thinker.

DUKE My decree...uh...ah...um...my decree is that everyone shall return here tomorrow to hear my next decree.

Herald plays fanfare.

BEATRICE That's the silliest decree I ever heard! Doesn't he know how silly he sounds?

STORYTELLER That's Beatrice, a girl who lives in the kingdom.

EMMYLOU Be easy on the duke, Beatrice. He's new at this, and he probably just couldn't think of anything to say.

STORYTELLER That's Emmylou, Beatrice's mom.

BEATRICE Why doesn't he decree something useful, like banning cell phones from ringing during church services?

SALLY Some people do strange things to make themselves feel important. Maybe the duke will relax into things soon. And the king and queen will be home from DragonLand before you know it. How much trouble can the duke stir up between now and then?

STORYTELLER That's Sally, Beatrice's mom.

BEATRICE Well, I can't wait to see what his decree will be tomorrow.

STORYTELLER The entire realm was as curious as Beatrice about the grand duke's decree. The next day, everyone in the royal kingdom returned to the royal balcony as decreed.

Extras and the Man join Beatrice, Emmylou, and Sally.

Some of them gathered out of obedience, some gathered out of curiosity about what the Grand Duke Dwayne would decree, and the rest of them gathered because they'd heard a rumor that the castle would be giving away free coffee. That last group was disappointed. There was no free coffee.

LEADER Maybe they accidentally overheard me when I invited the congregation to coffee hour.

STORYTELLER Right—that's probably where the miscommunication happened. Anyway, all the people listened expectantly as Grand Duke Dwayne strutted out onto the balcony and puffed up his chest.

Grand Duke Dwayne struts onto balcony. Herald joins him.

DUKE Hear ye, hear ye! [*looks around with satisfaction and arrogance*] I proclaim that too many jelly beans are being eaten. We could have a jelly bean shortage if we're not careful. Henceforth, no one shall eat jelly beans without royal permission. I also proclaim that you shall not request royal permission to eat jelly beans, as no one is getting permission to do so.

Herald plays fanfare.

STORYTELLER Everyone looked at each other, bewildered. The king and queen—who were currently happily frolicking at DragonLand—never made such silly proclamations. Could the duke possibly be serious?

MAN [*chuckles loudly, then guffaws*] Come on, Duke! We know you're just kidding. [*continues to laugh loudly*]

DUKE Silence! I am very serious. Anyone found eating jelly beans shall be beheaded. You shall all return in one week for my next proclamation.

STORYTELLER No one chuckled now. Everyone returned silently to their homes. Many shook their heads in dismay. But no one ate a single jelly bean.

All but the Leader and the Storyteller take their seats.

LEADER As we know, there are people in our own community who live without things that are much more important than jelly beans. Many of us can buy anything we want at the grocery store, or even at restaurants. However, we share our [town/city] with families who don't have enough food to eat, or whose poverty forces them to choose between buying food or medicine, or between milk and laundry soap. As we pause in our story, I invite you to sing "From You I Receive" as we bring forward canned goods for our local food bank. If you don't feel like walking your food offering forward, please hold it up. Children, if you want to help, would you please look for cans and boxes that need to be brought to our baskets?

"From You I Receive," *SLT,* 402

Adults and children bring food forward, putting it into large baskets, in an out-of-the-way but visible location at the front of the sanctuary.

LEADER Thank you for your many ways of giving to those in need, and thanks to our Storyteller for resuming the service.

STORYTELLER When the Not-so-grand Duke Dwayne outlawed jelly beans, it was a hard week in the kingdom—people had to turn to chocolate to satisfy their cravings for sweets. But they managed to get by without jelly beans somehow. One week later, as threatened—oops, I mean, as promised—the Grand Duke Dwayne stepped out onto the balcony to issue his next decree to a growing crowd, who wondered: Would the duke's next decree be as far-fetched?

As Grand Duke Dwayne and the Herald step forward, the other cast members gather once again to listen.

DUKE Hear ye, hear ye! [*exudes pompousness and imperialism*] Today I proclaim that too many children are being impertinent to their parents. I believe that children become sassy and disrespectful because of the books they read. I've taken it upon myself to compile a short list of books that are acceptable for children [*unrolls a long scroll*] and I have instructed the royal libraries to lock up all unapproved books. Therefore, and henceforth, no children shall be allowed to read books that have not received the royal seal of approval! All who disobey me shall lose their heads.

Herald plays fanfare, exits with Grand Duke Dwayne.

BEATRICE He's nuts!

SALLY I'm afraid that doesn't matter, sweetie. Until the king and queen return from DragonLand, the duke's word is the law.

EMMYLOU For now, we should go home and gather up our books to send to the castle for royal approval.

BEATRICE But Mo-o-o-o-o-om! What am I supposed to do without my books?

Emmylou and Sally soothe Beatrice. Then all cast members exit.

LEADER Some leaders rule by fear, using their authority to exert power over other people. As Unitarian Universalists, we are guided by love. We're guided by trusting one another to use power respectfully, and share it with others. We're guided by our desire to serve the common good. And so each week in our worship service, we invite love to guide us, and service to inspire us, by taking the time to listen to the joys and sorrows in our community. In this time, we ask you to come forward if you have a celebration or a sadness that you wish to share.

Joys and Sorrows

After the congregation has shared, the Leader calls for a period of silent meditation and allows at least a minute of silence.

LEADER Spirit of Love and Guidance,
in these quiet moments let us remember our power and our
  agency.
It is tempting, at times, to use our power to protect our own
  interests,

to wall off our hearts, to lift ourselves above others;
and each of us has done so, with or without awareness.
We remember that by serving you and one another,
we are called to use our power in a different way:
to be agents of healing in a hurting world,
to bring about justice, to give voice to hope, to summon forth
compassion.
Inspire us, Source of Love, to do all these things:
to heal, to help, to bless—and to do so with love.

"There Is More Love Somewhere," *SLT,* 95

Cast members return to the front.

STORYTELLER   As you recall, the citizens of the royal kingdom were beginning to feel upset, because the Grand Duke Dwayne had outlawed jelly beans and, as it turns out, all of the most interesting books. A week later, he issued yet another decree—this one more heavy-handed than the others. As always, the Duke puffed up his chest and strutted out onto the castle balcony.

DUKE   [*struts onto balcony*] Hear ye, hear ye! Since I grew up with just one mother and one father, and I turned out so well, I proclaim that this arrangement will work best for everyone. In one week, any children who have too many mothers or fathers, or not enough, will be thrown into the dungeon.

All cast members except the Duke gasp and pause for a moment of stunned silence. Herald plays an intentionally botched fanfare, perhaps approximating a raspberry.

BEATRICE   [*stricken, to Emmylou and Sally*] It wasn't that bad to give up my jelly beans. It was kind of bad to give up my favorite books. But I won't give you up. I won't! I have two mothers. Both of you are my moms, and I've turned out great! He can't throw me into the dungeon!

EMMYLOU   I'm afraid he can, technically, but we'll never let him take you away.

SALLY   Never! We'd run away to another kingdom first.

EMMYLOU   [*to Sally*] We should have gone to DragonLand ourselves, huh?

DUKE   Come back next week for another royal decree. [*begins to walk back into the castle, then stops and turns around*] Oh—in the meantime, don't forget about the jelly beans.

STORYTELLER   Throughout the village, everyone shook their heads in shock, murmuring about the lengths to which the Grand Duke Dwayne had taken his power.

Duke, still on balcony, takes out tabloid magazine, holding it so the cover is visible as he reads it.

While the duke squirreled himself away in his aunt and uncle's castle, studying important papers and composing his next decree, he seemed oblivious to the people's distress. He was certainly oblivious of their planning.

Duke exits. Beatrice and Dexter come to center of chancel, conferring.

The duke didn't know, for example, that later that evening after dinner, Beatrice had an emergency meeting with her friend Dexter. Like others in the kingdom, they felt indignant about the grand duke's most recent decree. Stirred into reflection and action, Beatrice and Dexter made a list.

BEATRICE   There's Daniel—he has two dads. That's one dad too many, according to Grand Duke Dweeb.

DEXTER   Don't forget about Anastasia. She lives with her grandparents.

BEATRICE   And what about Ezra? He has just one mom and no dads. The duke will take him away from his mom, too.

DEXTER   We love all of these people! We definitely have to do something to protect them.

STORYTELLER Soon Dexter and Beatrice had listed several other kids who did not have the right parents, according to the Grand Duke Dweeb—uh, sorry, I mean Dwayne—and who were in danger of being taken away from their parents. They were determined not to let their friends remain in this danger. The next day, all of the children met secretly, in the woods, with Dexter and Beatrice. Beatrice told them her plan.

Beatrice and Dexter huddle with a few children from among the congregation until the hymn begins.

LEADER As the children of the kingdom meet to create their plan, we remember the lands across the world where people are denied freedoms. We remember the lands where people are denied basic human rights. We remember the countries where justice and freedom have yet to take hold. With these members of the human family in our hearts, let us sing "This is My Song."

"This Is My Song," *SLT,* 159

STORYTELLER The following day, the grand duke again strutted out onto the balcony, eager to make his next proclamation. The people gathered below, ready to meet his royal decree with their plan, code named Rebellious Resistance to Royal Wrong-Headed Righteousness.

Grand Duke Dwayne struts onto balcony. Beatrice, Emmylou, Sally, Dexter and the Extras form the crowd. Extras and/or children join the crowd, if there's room, or stay in their seats to deliver their lines.

DUKE Hear ye, hear ye! It has come to my attention that someone in this kingdom found a jelly bean under their sofa cushion, and ate it—the jelly bean, not the sofa. You are in big trouble as soon as I find out who you are. It has also come to my attention that there is an unapproved book circulating among the kingdom. I remind you that you will be very sorry if you are caught reading Captain Underpants and the Wrath of the Wicked Wedgie-Woman.

STORYTELLER The duke's puffery made the kingdom's people even more determined to carry out their plan of rebellion.

DUKE   However, what troubles me most supremely is that a number of families in this royal kingdom are defying my proclamation that families must have exactly one mother and one father! Some of you children out there have two mothers, and one of you has a grandmother instead of two parents, and so on. Later this afternoon, my royal guards will seek out you children who are in such danger, and put you in the dungeon.

STORYTELLER   Suddenly, the grand duke heard voices rising from the crowd below.

EXTRA 1   Hear ye, hear ye! [*puffs up chest and stands on chair*] Henceforth, I proclaim that all pet goldfish must be potty-trained.

All cast members begin to giggle.

EXTRA 2   Hear ye, hear ye! [*pompously*] I'm very smart, and I believe it's because I eat my favorite sandwich every day for lunch: fried onion with grape jelly. I hereby decree that everyone must eat fried-onion-and-grape-jelly sandwiches at every meal.

Cast members shout general approval.

EXTRA 3   Hear ye, hear ye! [*puffed up*] I accidentally swallowed a grasshopper when I was two, and I turned out so well, I proclaim that all two-year-olds must swallow grasshoppers.

All cast members whoop with glee.

EXTRA 1   Hear ye, hear ye! [*arrogantly*] I proclaim that dogs are not allowed to burp.

STORYTELLER   As these proclamations rained down on him, the duke began to cringe. A look of uncertainty crossed his face, and he held up a hand . . .

Grand Duke Dwayne holds up his hand, opens his mouth, and stammers, but can't say a thing.

STORYTELLER   . . . but was speechless. The silly proclamations continued . . . [*invites proclamations from the congregation*]

LEADER Hear ye, hear ye! I proclaim that this is the best royal kingdom ever! I proclaim that when the king and queen return from DragonLand, they're going to be very proud of their people. And I proclaim that we must pause the story to receive this morning's offering. You know, these royal subjects may be having fun with the duke's proclamations, but they're doing more than that: they're creatively standing up to his unjust decrees and his ruling by fear! It wouldn't have been easy for just one person to do that on his or her own. The more we join together, the more our power counts. Let us remember that when we pool our creativity, we can overcome obstacles. When we pool our energy, we can make great things happen. And when we pool our resources, and share our gifts generously with this congregation, we support this community as well as Unitarian Universalism.

Crowd sits or waits quietly in place as offering is gathered.

Offering

The gathered crowd acts out the following scene, as described.

STORYTELLER Potty-trained goldfish. Fried-onion-and-grape-jelly sandwiches. Two-year-olds swallowing grasshoppers. No burping dogs. The silly proclamations continued, and soon every person in the kingdom was giggling or chuckling. They laughed so hard their sides hurt. And they couldn't stop. Soon everyone was rolling on the ground, giggling and laughing and chuckling, poking each other and laughing some more.

DEXTER [*stands up, puffs out chest*] I proclaim that giggling is against the law!

STORYTELLER Everyone roared with laughter . . . except for Grand Duke Dweeb.

DUKE Guards! Arrest everyone laughing! Off with their heads!

Guard sternly strides up the aisle, then dissolves into laughter.

STORYTELLER But the guards were laughing too.

GUARD   Off with their heads, off with their noses, send them to bed, without any toeses!

STORYTELLER   This was too much for the grand duke. He had never been so humiliated in all his life. They were laughing at him! And so, with his chest still puffed out as far as he could get it, the Grand Duke Dwayne strode off the balcony, down the castle stairs, and into his coach.

Grand Duke Dwayne makes a fast getaway.

He rode out of the kingdom as fast as he could, and was never seen or heard from again, except in his annual holiday card that he sent to his aunt and uncle. Just in case you're wondering, that evening, everyone ate jelly beans for dinner. And except for a few stomachaches that night, they all lived happily ever after.

LEADER   Let us again remember the importance of loving, and of holy boldness, by closing our service with "One More Step."

"One More Step," *SLT,* 168

LEADER   *From the words of Edward Everett Hale:*

I am only one
But still I am one.
I cannot do everything,
But still I can do something.
And because I cannot do everything
I will not refuse to do the
something I can do.

Let us each go out into the world, doing the "something" we can do, and confident that these small acts build upon each other to bring about peace, to create justice, and to spread love.

Babble

This service is loosely based on the story of the Tower of Babel, told in the book of Genesis. What happens when our ambition and greed overshadow our common purpose? What is the cost of seeking results over relationship? This story illustrates that, while we may get distracted by our ambition and greed, no success is very enjoyable without love and the warm spirit of community.

Preparation (moderate)

- Gather together a clipboard; blueprints (or any rolled up papers); "money"; lots of shoe boxes painted to look like bricks or cardboard toy bricks; a wheelbarrow; and hammers, saws, tape measures, and other simple construction tools. If your actors are comfortable in them and can find them, construction helmets are a great costume addition.

- Prepare a large box or block with a Styrofoam surface to serve as the cornerstone for the tower. Write or paint the word "COMMUNITY" on the front. It should be very large and visible.

- Recruit a volunteer to be pulled into the action from the pews.

- *Rehearsal will take about 2 hours.*

Roles (8–10, those who need to attend rehearsal are marked with *)

- Director (can also play any of the Villagers or the Worker)*
- Leader*
- Storyteller*

- Villager 1*
- Villager 2*
- Villager 3*
- Worker
- 2–3 Extra Villagers*

As the service opens, the Director paces in front of the sanctuary, muttering to herself in a businesslike way and looking at her clipboard. The Leader stands nearby and watches.

DIRECTOR   Piano player—check!
   Ushers at the doors—check!
   Microphones on—check!
   Cell phone off—check!
   Papers in order—check!

[*to the congregation*] How about all of you? Do you have your orders of service and hymnals ready? C'mon, people—get your act together! We have a worship service to kick off. Let's go, people; let's go, go, go!

LEADER   [*calmly*] How're you doing, [*Director's name*]?

DIRECTOR   Fine. I'm just trying to get this show on the road.

LEADER   Would you mind if I give it a go? I mean, you're certainly efficient, and I appreciate your commitment to making sure our worship service runs smoothly. But it's okay if some things aren't exactly right. Personally, I think it's a little more important that we enjoy each other's companionship today, and that people know how glad we are to see them. If it's alright with you, I'd love to begin with a little welcome instead of your checklist.

Director indicates that's fine, and sits down.

Welcome

The Leader welcomes congregants and visitors.

LEADER This morning we'll be treated to a great story for all ages, about working together. [*pauses and looks at Director*] How am I doing?

Director gives the Leader a big thumbs up, and a "keep going" sign.

In this congregation, we enjoy the diversity that comes from having members of many ages, beliefs, languages, and heritages. Although we don't all believe the same things about God and Mystery and the Universe, one thing we do agree on is that walking together in love is more important than any one thing we do, or any accomplishment we might achieve.

As we enter into worship, put away the pressures of the world that ask us to perform, to take up masks, to put on brave fronts—silence the voices that ask you to be perfect. This is a community of compassion and welcoming. You do not have to do anything to earn the love contained within these walls. You do not have to be braver, smarter, stronger, or better than you are in this moment to belong here with us. You have only to bring the gift of your body, no matter how able; your seeking mind, no matter how busy; and your animal heart, no matter how broken. Bring all that you are, and all that you love, to this hour. Let us worship together.

Chalice Lighting

"Let It Be a Dance," *SLT,* 311

STORYTELLER That hymn has a beautiful message: We're here for one another in the good times and the bad times, too—it's all part of the dance we do together. Ric Masten's words, "If nothing's wrong, then nothing's right," remind me of a story about a village that had to relearn that lesson. I think you'd enjoy that story. Would you like to hear it?

A number of years ago, in a land nowhere near where we're gathered, there was a village of farmers and shepherds. Just about everyone in the village knew everyone else, and they all liked each other very much. Each day was a new opportunity to say hello, to exchange news, and to give thanks for living among friendly neighbors.

Villagers 1 and 2 enter and greet each other warmly.

VILLAGER 1   Morning, neighbor!

VILLAGER 2   Good Morning!

STORYTELLER   In fact, the farmers and the shepherds and the children of the valley enjoyed each others' company so much that they hungered for a place to spend time together as a group. No one's home or barn was large enough to hold all of the villagers. The pastures weren't very comfortable meeting places, either; it was important to have a gathering place that was free from rain and wind and sheep droppings.

VILLAGER 1   [*to Villager 2*] Look out for the shee—never mind.

Several Villagers enter and pantomime conversation, acting out the following.

STORYTELLER   All of the villagers dreamed of the day when they'd be able to gather under a single roof, for any number of reasons: to meet for business, or to watch their children play together, or to enjoy feasts and music, or just to sit and watch a fire in the fireplace. So strong were these dreams, and their longing to bring those dreams into being, that the people of the village decided to build a tower—a beautiful, gleaming tower that would be visible from every corner of the village.

VILLAGERS   [*chanting*] Tow-er! Tow-er! Tow-er! Tow-er! [*put on construction helmets, unroll blueprints, and tote in a wheelbarrow full of bricks*]

STORYTELLER   Soon enough, the villagers were drafting plans and pooling their resources to buy bricks and other supplies for construction. The site for the new tower was cleared, the workers assigned, and the blueprints drawn up. But before the builders laid the first bricks onto the tower's base, they gathered the people of the village around.

VILLAGER 3   Friends, before we build the walls of our tower, let us remember why we've undertaken this project. This tower will be a home for our entire community, a hearth to which all are welcome, a shelter from the cold winds, and a haven from the storms of the world. This tower will belong to all of us, just as we all help with its construction. As we build, may we be guided by the spirit of . . . community!

Villagers lay down the large box or block as the cornerstone of the tower. Villager 3 "engraves"—in quick pantomime, as the word will already have been prepared —the cornerstone with the word Community.

VILLAGERS   [*happily*] Community! [*after a brief pause*] Tow-er! Tow-er! Tow-er! Tow-er! [*invite the congregation to chant along*]

As the chant quiets, the actors take their seats.

LEADER   What wonderful news for the people of the village! They dreamed of building their own gathering space, and their new tower was on its way to being built. What could possibly go wrong? I don't know how this story will unfold, but I do know that all communities—whether in far-away, long-ago villages or right here in [name of city/town]—are visited by both joy and sorrow. Whether we expect it or not, the members of this congregation will always have things to celebrate and things to mourn. Today we share our joys and sorrows in the spirit of community, knowing that this congregation offers its healing listening in response to our sorrows, and joyful hearts in response to our celebrations.

Joys and Sorrows

After the congregation has shared, the Leader calls for a period of silent meditation and allows at least a minute of silence.

"There's a River Flowin' in My Soul," *STJ,* 1007

Actors take their places at the front again.

STORYTELLER   Since we last saw our villagers, a lot has happened. They spent many busy weeks constructing their new tower, and the gleaming walls quickly rose above the green fields. Just as they'd planned, the tower was visible from every corner of the village. Its construction was nearly complete; soon the villagers would have the gathering place they'd dreamed of.

VILLAGERS   [*chanting, happily*] Tow-er! Tow-er! Tow-er! Tow-er! [*again invite the congregation to join in the chanting*]

STORYTELLER   A funny thing happened, though. Do you remember what was carved on the tower's cornerstone? [*waits for someone in the congregation to say "community"*] Community! But notice what they're still talking about: the tower! In fact, the taller and more impressive the tower's walls grew, the more the villagers became transfixed by what they had achieved.

VILLAGER 1   Not too shabby, huh?

VILLAGER 2   We are totally awesome! We rock!

STORYTELLER   As pride in their tower grew, a new idea began circulating among the members of the village.

VILLAGER 1   This tower looks so great, maybe we should give up farming and sheepherding and just concentrate on building stuff.

VILLAGER 2   Definitely!

Villagers 1 and 2 work busily, pantomiming making other smaller towers, each oblivious to the other, while the Storyteller speaks.

STORYTELLER   And so, seduced by their creation, the villagers decided to keep building—and it turns out they were pretty good at it. They took to building like ducks to water, like sheep to pasture. Three things quickly became evident—at least, to observers, since the villagers were too busy building to notice. First, not everyone shared the same vision of what new building should go where, or for what purpose. For example, one villager began to lay a new foundation and build new walls in one corner of a field, without noticing that a neighboring builder was working nearby, just as busily. Eventually, someone noticed.

VILLAGER 3 [*to Villager 2*] Hey! What's that you're working on?

VILLAGER 2 A warm, sturdy stable for all of the village livestock.

VILLAGER 3 [*to Villager 1*] And what's that you're working on?

VILLAGER 1 [*crestfallen*] I'm building... um... a warm, sturdy stable for all of the village livestock.

VILLAGER 2 Oh, great! We don't need two stables. Now what are we going to do?

Villagers 1 and 2 leave, quietly squabbling and gesticulating.

STORYTELLER Besides the fact that individual building projects were developing willy-nilly, a second fact became clear: the more sophisticated and ambitious their construction became, the more the villagers needed outside help to complete the technical details of the new buildings.

Worker enters, wearing a sophisticated tool belt or other gadgetry and referring to blueprints.

WORKER [*briskly*] See, you put the exwhumpilator into the bifurcatory split valve, but only after you seal off the inducillation jibrialle. Got it?

VILLAGER 3 ... um ... well ... if you say so.

WORKER C'mon—who doesn't know how to seal off an inducillation jibrialle? It's even easier than jump-circuiting the plonjib on a whizgametz!

Villager 3 stares at Worker, speechless.

WORKER [*holding out a palm*] That'll be 245 shillings, please.

Villager 3 pays Worker as they exit. The rest of the Villagers stay up front and, with tools, continue to act out the following scene as it's described.

STORYTELLER   So the villagers began to feel the pinch of hiring outside help to construct their fancy buildings that were being built hither and yon. These were simple farmers and sheepherders, remember, without many resources—but they kept spending their hard-earned and carefully saved shillings on building materials and advice from experts. And what effect do you imagine that had on their flocks of sheep, and fields of grain and produce? [*takes ideas from the congregation*]

I'll tell you: The fields and pastures went to seed, and all the livestock were neglected. That was the third great cost of the villagers' building frenzy. But those villagers kept building. They sawed and hammered, sanded and painted. Eventually, they put exwhumpilators into bifurcatory split valves (but only after sealing off inducillation jibrialles). After a while, the builders of the village constructed more and more buildings. They created hallways and balustrades, columns and cupolas, steeples and friezes. The more the villagers built, the more their appetite for building increased. Before long, all of the children's school lessons were suspended so that every able-bodied person could work on the buildings—everyone from six years old to one hundred and six years old.

VILLAGER 2   [*standing over a member of the congregation*] Here's another one! She looks strong! [*pulls the new cast member into the action*]

STORYTELLER   What's more, the wings of the different buildings soon sprawled across the hillside, and the workers were so busy and so far apart that they couldn't hear one another anymore.

Villagers 1 and 2 shout the following lines to each other across the sanctuary.

VILLAGER 1   Hey! Do you think we need more paint?

VILLAGER 2   No, it doesn't look like rain!

STORYTELLER   The more scattered the workers were, the more confusing their communication became.

Worker and Villagers shout the following lines back and forth across the sanctuary.

EXTRA   Please tell Gladys that we need to widen the doorway to fit her tuba in here.

VILLAGER 1   Tell Gladys to go through the door and sit with her tuba in there.

VILLAGER 2   Tell Gladys that her tube of toothpaste is in there.

VILLAGER 3   Hey, Gladys—you can brush your teeth now.

LEADER   [*to congregation*] This sounds like one confused village to me. [*to Villagers*] Excuse me, villagers, but please remind me: why are you building all of this stuff?

ALL VILLAGERS   Because we can!

Actors take their seats.

LEADER   Because they can? The farmers are neglecting their fields and sheep; they're fraying their friendships; they're raiding their saved-up resources . . . but their original guiding principle was community. Now it's building, building, building. I don't know about you, but it seems to me that the villagers had a vision—to create a place where they could enjoy being together—and instead got carried away by their own ambition. There's a difference between communities that are sustained by a shared vision, and communities that are overtaken by separate visions. In this Unitarian Universalist congregation, our shared vision is one of a world filled with peace, justice, compassion, and hope. We believe that we're co-creators, and co-shapers of this world, and that together we can bring it into being. Part of our call is to work together. Each week when we take the offering, it's a chance for us to remember the power of our community, and the power of our resources. The act of putting money in the basket is a simple but powerful gesture: the embodiment of our belief in generosity. Thank you for taking part in this symbolic act this morning, and for giving in the name of community.

Offering

All Villagers return to their places at their "construction" sites.

STORYTELLER As you recall, things were getting a little confused in the village, as their sprawl of buildings became more important than being together, as their resources were spent on making their buildings go higher and higher, and as their frenzied work habits led to poor communication. Before you could say "exwhumpilator," there were more signs that bricks, lumber, and stones had become more important than people.

Villager 1 walks past, carrying an armful of bricks. She stumbles and falls, dropping the bricks on the ground, and cries out in pain.

VILLAGER 2 Hey! Watch your step. Those bricks are expensive.

VILLAGER 1 [*stricken, clutching leg*] Um, I'm just going to go sit down for a while. I'm fine! Thanks for asking . . . [*limps off to a corner to sit, clearly hurt*]

Villager 2 is too busy re-stacking the bricks to see Villager 1 limp away. Villager 3 whistles or shouts to get everyone's attention. The actors freeze and look at Villager 3.

VILLAGER 3 Gather 'round, people—someone just got hurt! Is there a doctor or nurse anywhere?

VILLAGER 2 Nope. They're all a half-mile away, sealing off the inducillation jibrialles on Building 47. They're way too busy to provide medical care.

VILLAGER 3 What are we doing?

VILLAGER 2 Building.

VILLAGER 3 No, no—I mean, why? For what? First someone gets hurt and we're worried about the bricks . . . and then we're too busy building to help her? That's not right. When did building and buying bricks become more important than the people in this village? Do you remember how all of these building projects began?

VILLAGER 2 With the tower.

VILLAGERS (NOT #3) [*chanting, happily*] Tow-er! Tow-er! Tow-er! Tow-er!

VILLAGER 3 Hush! Stop with the tower, already!

Villagers look confused.

VILLAGER 3 Listen, I love our tower too. In fact, I'm proud of all forty-seven of our buildings and how beautifully we've constructed them. But do you remember what life was like before all of this . . . building stuff began? Do you remember what we wrote on the cornerstone of our tower? [*to congregation*] Please . . . please . . . remind them why we built the tower to begin with.

The Storyteller leads the congregation in chanting "Community! Community! Community!"

VILLAGER 1 You know, I remember how great it was to spend the day in my fields, and come home to see all of you.

VILLAGER 2 And I remember how we dreamed of a wonderful life, with a beautiful building to gather in, all together. We never meant to build up our land, ignore our livelihoods, and forget our friendships.

VILLAGER 3 Sustaining our friendships—our community—was the whole point of this!

VILLAGERS Community . . . Community!

Villagers embrace warmly.

STORYTELLER And that's where the building stopped. It simply stopped. The villagers set down their tools, returned to their fields, and reconnected with one another. For many years, the beautiful tower offered shelter to everyone in the village. Indeed, it became the gathering place—the hearth—that they had intended it to be. But every single time a villager entered or exited that tower, he or she looked down at the cornerstone, where a single word glowed up at them and reminded them of what they had nearly lost beneath the crush of building. That word continued to guide the village for years to come. The word was . . . [*gestures congregation to answer*]

CONGREGATION   Community!

DIRECTOR   [*walks down aisle with clipboard, approvingly*] Community—check! That's a wrap, folks!

LEADER   Let us sing of our own commitment to one another, and to the human family around the world. Please join me in our closing hymn, "Building a New Way."

"Building a New Way," *STJ,* 1017

LEADER   Let us, too, build a new way, friends:
The way of peace,
the way of freedom and hope.
Let us build a world of compassion and justice—
And let us do so together,
in the common language of love.

Benediction

The words on these pages are simply ideas, waiting to be spun to life through your creativity and faith. They're the raw material for spiritual exploration and community-building. And they're *yours*.

As you bring these stories into being, may your energy and efforts be met with gladness;

may your playfulness and inspiration flow with ease, and delight others;

and may your passion for Unitarian Universalism be a spark of transformation within your own heart, in your congregation, and in the larger world.